Test Best®
for
Success

Reading and
Language Arts

LEVEL
I

STECK-VAUGHN

A Harcourt Company

www.steck-vaughn.com

ACKNOWLEDGMENTS

Contributing Author

Susan Luton

Illustrations

C J Hepburn

Photo Credits

p.6a ©Paul A. Souders/CORBIS; p.6b ©Reuters NewMedia Inc./CORBIS; p.11 ©Galen Rowell/CORBIS; p.18 ©Bettmann/CORBIS; p.39a Courtesy of Nebraska State Historical Society; p.39b ©Bettmann/CORBIS; p.44 ©Brian Vikander/CORBIS; p.45 ©Bettmann/CORBIS; p.51 Courtesy of Nebraska State Historical Society.

Additional photography by Corbis Royalty Free and Getty Royalty Free.

Steck-Vaughn is indebted to the following for permission to use material in this book:

"Cameras Help Teenagers Look Beyond Bitter Conflicts" by Joel Greenberg from *The New York Times*, February 24, 2000. Copyright © 2000 by the New York Times Co. Reprinted by permission.

"About Antarctica" from *TIME for Kids* magazine, August 11th, 2000. Used with permission from *TIME for Kids* magazine Copyright © 2000, 2001.

"A Look Back at Antarctica" from *TIME for Kids* magazine, October 18th, 2000. Used with permission from *TIME for Kids* magazine Copyright © 2000, 2001.

"Can Milk Make You Happy? Can Fish Make You Smart?" by Faith Hickman Brynie. Excerpted from *ODYSSEY's* October 2000 issue: *Eat Up! Eat Smart!* Copyright © 2000, Cobblestone Publishing Company, 30 Grove Street, Suite C, Peterborough, NH 03458. All Rights Reserved. Reprinted by permission of the publisher.

"For the Love of Animals: An Interview with Vegetarian and Moosewood Cookbook Author Susan Harville" by Barbara Eaglesham from *ODYSSEY's* October 2000 issue: *Eat Up! Eat Smart!* Copyright © 2000, Cobblestone Publishing Company, 30 Grove Street, Suite C, Peterborough, NH 03458. All Rights Reserved. Reprinted by permission of the publisher.

ISBN 0-7398-6712-1

Copyright ©2003 Steck-Vaughn Company

1 2 3 4 5 6 7 8 9 021 08 07 06 05 04 03 02

Test Best® for Success, Reading and Language Arts, Level I

Table of Contents

Strategies

Reading Comprehension: Test-Taking Strategies

Section I: Three Levels of Comprehension s5

Section II: The Three Strategies s6

Strategy 1: The Check and See Strategy s6

Strategy 2: The Puzzle Piece Strategy s8

Strategy 3: The What Lights Up Strategy s12

Reading Comprehension: Modeled Instruction s14

Basic Understanding

Objective 1: Indicating Sequence of Events s15

Objective 1: Defining Vocabulary s17

Analyze Text

Objective 2: Identifying Theme and Story Elements s19

Objective 2: Drawing Conclusions s20

Objective 2: Inferring Relationships s22

Evaluate and Extend Meaning

Objective 3: Making Predictions s23

Objective 3: Judging Author Purpose, Point of View, and Effectiveness s24

Identify Reading Strategies

Objective 4: Summarizing Content s25

Objective 4: Using Graphics and Text Structure s26

Test Practice: Skill Building

Unit 1: Reading

Lesson 1: Reading Comprehension 4

Unit 1 Test 9

Unit 2: Language Arts

Lesson 2: Sentence Structure 13

Lesson 3: Writing Strategies 15

Lesson 4: Editing Skills 17

Unit 2 Test 19

Comprehensive Test: Reading and Language Arts 23

Part 1 25

Part 2 39

Student Answer Sheet 63

TO THE TEACHER

Test Best for Success is an instructional series for you to use with your students. As teachers, you know that children learn best by doing. Therefore, we have developed a series that will actively involve your students while they learn and apply specific strategies in answering questions about what they have read. Specific learning strategies will be presented through modeling and practice. Varying degrees of support, structure, and explanation are provided.

Many genres, such as fiction, nonfiction, poems, fables, and folk tales are included. Some of the passages are taken from published, authentic literature reflecting the type of instruction that exists in classrooms today. The questions following each passage reflect different levels of comprehension. The material in this book provides your students with step-by-step instruction that will maximize their reading success in classroom work as well as in testing situations.

Test-Taking Strategies

Three specific strategies, which are designed to assist the students in answering questions, are presented here.

Modeled Instruction

Instruction and practice are provided for specific assessment objectives.

Test Practice

Students have the opportunity to practice all the strategies that they have learned. This section can be used to simulate tests. It may be used to evaluate students' progress and to assess further needs.

Reading Comprehension: Test-Taking Strategies

Section I:

Three Levels of Comprehension
There are three levels of comprehension.

Level 1: Basic Understanding
This is called the literal level of comprehension. It is also called recalling information. **The facts you need to know are written in the story.** If you look at the story you will see the information that you need.

Level 2: Analyzing information
This is called the interpretive level of comprehension. It is also called constructing meaning. **This is using the information that you read in the story and figuring out what it means.** You use the facts you read and decide how they go together. This level also involves analyzing form. This is when you analyze the parts that make up a story or the story type.

Level 3: Evaluating and Extending information
This is called the critical level of comprehension. It is also called extending and evaluating meaning. **This is thinking about the story and adding what you know from your own experiences.** You may also think about what the author meant.

Section II:

The Three Strategies

There are three strategies you can use to help you answer questions.

STRATEGY 1

The CHECK AND SEE Strategy

The **Check and See Strategy** can be used when a question asks you to remember a fact from the story. The answer to the question is right there in the passage. It is not hidden. Some of the same words may be in the story and in the question.

 Check and See will help you answer *remembering information* questions.

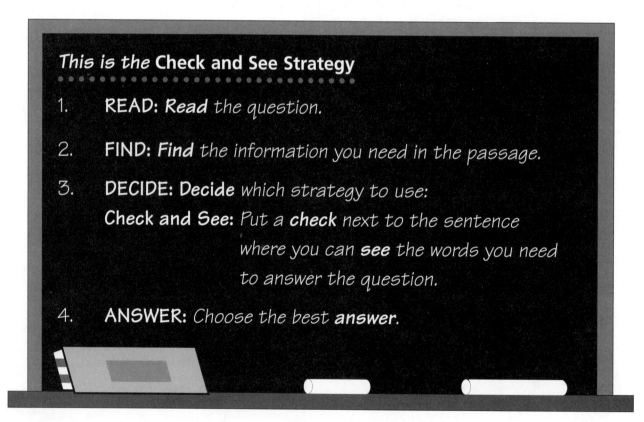

This is the **Check and See Strategy**

1. READ: *Read the question.*

2. FIND: *Find the information you need in the passage.*

3. DECIDE: *Decide which strategy to use:*
   Check and See: *Put a* **check** *next to the sentence where you can* **see** *the words you need to answer the question.*

4. ANSWER: *Choose the best* **answer**.

GUIDED INSTRUCTION: *Here is a story with a question using the* **Check and See Strategy**. *You do this one.*

When students search for an answer to a science problem, they use the scientific method. They learn to state the problem and gather information. After that, they form a hypothesis, which is a guess as to the solution to the problem. Next, an experiment is done and information is recorded and analyzed. Finally, a conclusion is reached. The scientific method is a procedure that students will use over and over again. It is an orderly and systematic way to solve a problem.

 What is the scientific method?

- A.   a guess to solve a problem
- B.   an orderly and systematic way to solve a problem
- C.   a very important science experiment
- D.   information that is recorded and analyzed

 Using the Check and See Strategy:

1.   **READ:** *Read the question.*

2.   **FIND:** *Find the information you need in the passage.*

3.   **DECIDE:** *Decide which strategy to use.* **Check and See:** *Put a check next to the sentence in the passage.*

4.   **ANSWER:** *Choose the best answer.*

The best answer is _____.

STRATEGY 2

The PUZZLE PIECE Strategy

The **Puzzle Piece Strategy** is another strategy you can use. Sometimes you may be asked a question that does not seem to have an answer. The answer is not right there in the story for you to see.

 Puzzle Piece is a strategy you can use when you must fit pieces of information together to get the answer. This is like putting a puzzle together. Puzzles are made up of several pieces. You cannot look at one piece and know what the picture is. Only when you put the puzzle pieces together can you see the whole picture.

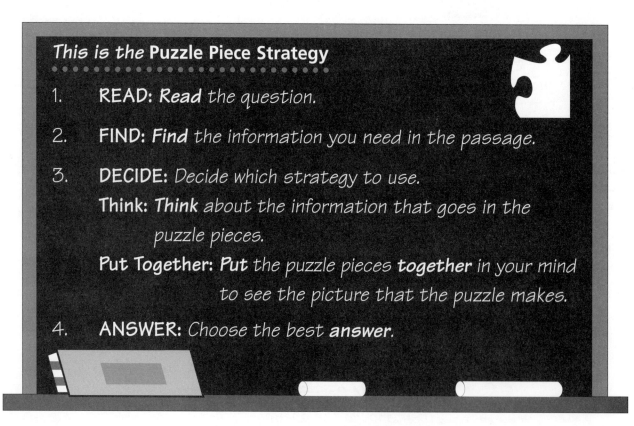

This is the **Puzzle Piece Strategy**

1. READ: *Read the question.*

2. FIND: *Find the information you need in the passage.*

3. DECIDE: *Decide which strategy to use.*
   Think: *Think about the information that goes in the puzzle pieces.*
   Put Together: *Put the puzzle pieces together in your mind to see the picture that the puzzle makes.*

4. ANSWER: *Choose the best answer.*

Constructing Meaning

Use the **Puzzle Piece Strategy** to answer questions that ask about the main idea, the best title for a story, or what the story is mostly about. It can also be used to answer questions that ask about what might happen next or what the author's purpose is. These kinds of questions are called *constructing meaning* questions.

 MODELED INSTRUCTION: *Here is a story for you to read. See how the* **Puzzle Piece Strategy** *is used.*

Many of the types of food we eat in our school cafeteria originated in other countries. The most popular lunch is pizza, which originally came from Italy. A Mexican favorite of many of our students is tacos. They are easy to make and fun to eat. A new addition in our cafeteria is egg rolls. These came from China. Another favorite is frankfurters. Many people think that franks are an American food. That is not true. Where do you think they came from?

 What is the best title for this selection?
- A. "All American Foods"
- B. "Friday Is Pizza Day"
- C. "International Lunches"
- D. "Mexican Favorites"

 Using the **Puzzle Piece Strategy**

1. **READ:** *Read the question.*

2. **FIND:** *Find the information you need.*

3. **DECIDE:** *Decide which strategy to use.*

4. **ANSWER:** *Choose the best answer.* Foods from many countries are found in the cafeteria.
The best answer is C: *"International Lunches"*

Analyzing Form

You can also use the **Puzzle Piece Strategy** to answer questions that ask about the parts that make up a story. The parts of a story are the *characters, setting, plot,* and *mood.*

Characters

- the people, animals, or things the story is about

Setting

- where and when the story takes place

Plot

- all the events that happen in the story

Mood

- the main feeling in the story

The **Puzzle Piece Strategy** is a strategy you can also use to answer questions that ask about what kind of story you have read. *Is it a fable, mystery, biography, or other type?*

Questions about how stories are put together or their type are called *analyzing form* questions. The **Puzzle Piece Strategy** can be used to answer all of these questions.

GUIDED INSTRUCTION: Here is another story for you to read with a question needing the **Puzzle Piece Strategy**. *Do this one on your own.*

This year in school I learned about the history of New England, a part of the United States. Most of what I learned I read from books and listening to my teacher. My family decided to take a vacation during the summer. Mom and Dad wanted to go to New England. They thought it would be a stimulating place to go on vacation. They thought I would enjoy seeing some of the places I learned about in school. I could not get that enthusiastic about seeing the educational sights of New England. I wasn't sure if this was the place where I wanted to go on vacation. New England didn't seem all that great to me. I thought the trip would be dull and boring.

 How does the writer feel about the trip?

- A. excited and anxious
- B. concerned but hopeful
- C. eager and ungrateful
- D. unenthusiastic and doubtful

Using the **Puzzle Piece Strategy**

1. **READ:** *Read the question.*

2. **FIND:** *Find the information you need in the passage.*

Hint: Questions about how a person feels in a story are asking about the mood.

3. **DECIDE:** *Decide which strategy to use.*

4. **ANSWER:** *Choose the best answer.*

The best answer is _____.

Strategy 3

What Lights Up is another strategy you can use when the answer is not right there. This time you add information from your own experiences.

What Lights Up can help you decide if something is important, true, real, useful, or a fact in the story. It can help you decide what would happen if the story went on or the ending was different.

You can use the **What Lights Up Strategy** to help you answer the hardest type of question. This is when you are asked to read and think beyond what is written. These questions are called *extending and evaluating meaning* questions.

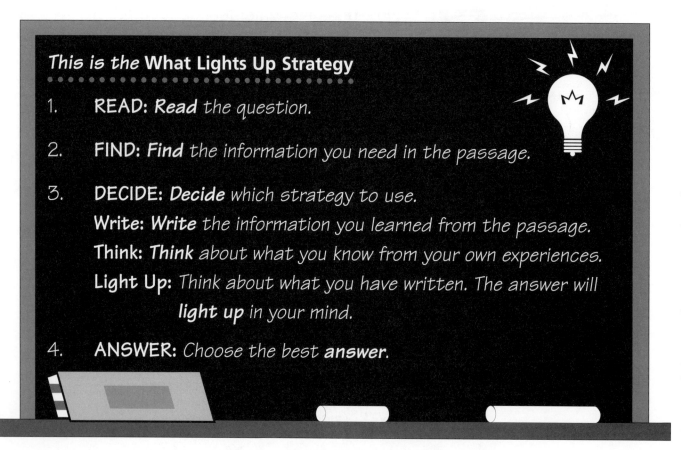

This is the **What Lights Up Strategy**

1. **READ:** *Read* the question.

2. **FIND:** *Find* the information you need in the passage.

3. **DECIDE:** *Decide* which strategy to use.
   Write: *Write* the information you learned from the passage.
   Think: *Think* about what you know from your own experiences.
   Light Up: *Think about what you have written. The answer will* **light up** *in your mind.*

4. **ANSWER:** *Choose the best* **answer**.

Do you know Aesop's fable about the fox and the grapes? One hot summer's day a fox was walking in the woods. He was very tired and very hungry but most of all he was thirsty. He suddenly saw a bunch of fat, juicy purple grapes hanging from a vine high above his head. He tried to reach the grapes but could not. He stepped back and took a running jump, but failed again. Finally, he stopped trying. As he walked away he said, "Who wants those grapes, anyway? They are probably sour."

With which sentence would the fox probably agree?

 A. Slow and steady wins the race.

 B. Do not try for grapes that are hard to reach.

 C. If you do not succeed, try again.

 D. What is hard to obtain is worthless.

Using the **What Lights Up Strategy**

1. **READ:** Read the question.

2. **FIND:** Find the information you need in the passage.

3. **DECIDE:** Decide which strategy to use.
Write: Write the information you learned from the passage.
Think: Think about what you know from your own experiences. Write that information.
Light Up: Think about what you have written. The answer will light up in your mind.

4. **ANSWER:** Choose the best answer.

The best answer is _____.

Reading Comprehension

Objectives

Objective 1: Basic Understanding

Demonstrate understanding of the literal meaning of a passage through identifying stated information, indicating sequence of events, and defining vocabulary.

Objective 2: Analyze Text

Demonstrate comprehension by drawing conclusions; inferring relationships such as cause and effect; and identifying theme and story elements such as plot, climax, character, and setting.

Objective 3: Evaluate and Extend Meaning

Demonstrate critical understanding by making predictions; distinguishing between fact and opinion, and reality and fantasy; transferring ideas to other situations; and judging author purpose, point of view, and effectiveness.

Objective 4: Identify Reading Strategies

Demonstrate awareness of techniques that enhance comprehension, such as using existing knowledge, summarizing content, comparing information across texts, using graphics and text structure, and formulating questions that deepen understanding.

Objective 1: Indicating Sequence of Events

Sometimes it is helpful to arrange events in the order they happened. This may help you to understand the passage better.

Sending mail by air began long before the Wright brothers invented the airplane. Pigeons carried army messages at the time of the Roman Empire, and balloons flew mail out of Paris, France, during the Franco-Prussian War in 1870. The first time an airplane transported mail was in India in February 1911.

Air mail began in North America in September 1911. Earle Ovington carried letters in his plane from Garden City Estates, New York, to Jamaica, New York. The occasion was the International Aviation Meet in Garden City Estates. After this, local people paid pilots to carry cards, letters, or souvenirs to nearby towns. People used this type of air mail as an entertainment rather than as a part of the regular mail delivery system.

The improvement of the airplane during World War I was significant in starting regular air mail service. Prior to the war, the planes were small and unreliable, and pilots often had to carry the mail on their knees.

Official air mail service began in North America on May 3, 1918. On that date, the U.S. War Department directed the Army Air Service to begin aerial mail service between Washington, D.C., and New York City six days a week. Beginning on May 15, 1918, the mail delivery began but got off to a rocky start. For example, pilots were inexperienced with flying cross-country, and planes crashed. After working out these problems, on August 12, 1918, airplanes and pilots from the U.S. Post Office officially replaced those from the Army Air Service, and air mail service was underway.

1 **On approximately what date did the local people pay pilots to carry their mail to nearby towns?**

   A February 11, 1911

   B September 15, 1911

   C May 3, 1918

   D August 3, 1918

   Hint: Write down the sequence of events.

2 **How was air mail first carried according to this text?**

   F By balloons

   G On airplanes

   H By pigeons

   J On Army planes

   Hint: Read the first paragraph.

3 **What happened first?**

   A The mail got lost.

   B Inexperienced pilots delivered the mail cross-country.

   C Airplanes and pilots from the U.S. Post Office replaced those from the Army Air Service.

   D The U.S. War Department directed the Army Air Service to begin aerial mail.

   Hint: You need to read all four paragraphs.

4 **When did regular mail delivery begin?**

   F when Earle Ovington carried letters from Garden City New York

   G during the Franco-Prussian War

   H when people paid pilots to deliver items as an entertainment

   J when the Army Service delivered mail six days a week

   Hint: Find the paragraph that talks about the regular mail delivery.

Answers

1 Ⓐ Ⓑ Ⓒ Ⓓ   3 Ⓐ Ⓑ Ⓒ Ⓓ

2 Ⓕ Ⓖ Ⓗ Ⓙ   4 Ⓕ Ⓖ Ⓗ Ⓙ

Objective 1: Indicating Sequence of Events

Written instructions tell the reader how to do something. To follow them means to do them in the same order in which they were written.

Mauricio is in his senior year of high school and is thinking about applying to West College. Students who wish to attend West College should complete the following steps. First, visit the college and tour the campus. Then, schedule a visit to the department in which you plan to major. Once you decide you want to apply, complete the application and mail it, along with the appropriate application fee, no later than January 15. If you are accepted, select the type of housing you want and send in your deposit to hold the room. Deposits received by May 15 will guarantee campus housing.

5   **When should Mauricio schedule a visit to the department in which he plans to major?**

A   After he selects the type of housing he wants

B   After he sends in a room deposit

C   Before he sends in his application

D   Before a tour of the campus

Hint: Write down the sequence of events.

6   **According to the passage, when is the application deadline?**

F   Immediately after a tour of the campus

G   January 15

H   May 15

J   There is no deadline.

Hint: Read the entire passage.

Many pests such as mice or insects, enter homes through cracks or holes in the foundation or siding. Other openings where pests might enter a house are through attic vents, outdoor water faucets, door frames, or electric, phone, and cable wires. There are a number of steps to take to prevent pests from invading your home. The first step is to examine the foundation and siding for cracks. Be especially careful to note hairline cracks. These often occur as the house ages and settles. Then, look carefully at where electrical, telephone, and TV cable lines enter the house. Finally, see if there are cracks around the doors and windows. Seal all openings with caulk or weatherstripping.

7   **What is the first place you should examine if you find pests in your house?**

A   Where the electrical wires enter the house

B   The foundation of the house

C   The roof

D   The vents

Hint: The first step is in the beginning of the paragraph.

8   **If you do have pests in your house, where should you look after checking the electrical, telephone, and TV cable lines?**

F   the siding

G   doors and windows

H   attic and roof vents

J   the foundation

Hint: Read the entire passage.

Answers

5   Ⓐ Ⓑ Ⓒ Ⓓ   7   Ⓐ Ⓑ Ⓒ Ⓓ

6   Ⓕ Ⓖ Ⓗ Ⓙ   8   Ⓕ Ⓖ Ⓗ Ⓙ

Objective 1: Defining Vocabulary

A word can have different meanings depending on when and how you use it. Readers can figure out the correct meaning of a word by reading the sentences around it.

Beethoven created many <u>instrumental</u> compositions. One of his most famous compositions is the Fifth Symphony.

9   **In this paragraph, <u>instrumental</u> means —**

   A   music created to be sung.

   B   intelligent.

   C   long.

   D   written for musical instruments.

Hint: Both sentences tell you what Beethoven composed.

Thomas Jefferson played an <u>instrumental</u> part in drafting the Declaration of Independence. The entire document was written almost totally by him.

10   **In this paragraph, <u>instrumental</u> means —**

   F   musical.

   G   insignificant.

   H   helpful.

   J   ineffective.

Hint: The second sentence explains Jefferson's role in writing the Declaration of Independence.

Harry had broken his leg and was in the hospital for a month. He was getting tired of lying around doing nothing. Whenever he tried to get out of bed, the nurse would tell him that he cannot get up on his own. He complained to her that he was not an <u>invalid</u>.

11   **In this passage, an <u>invalid</u> means —**

   A   someone who is not valid.

   B   a person who complains a lot.

   C   someone who gets into an accident.

   D   a weak, sickly person.

Hint: The third sentence helps explain the meaning of the word.

Chandra was excited because the coat she had wanted was finally on sale. However, she was unable to buy it because her credit card had expired and now was <u>invalid</u>.

12   **In this passage, the word <u>invalid</u> means —**

   F   issued to the wrong person.

   G   a good roommate.

   H   not in effect.

   J   penniless.

Hint: Read the whole sentence to find out what <u>invalid</u> means.

Objective 1: Defining Vocabulary

Prefixes and suffixes are parts of some words. A *prefix* appears at the beginning of a word. A *suffix* appears at the end of a word. Both prefixes and suffixes affect the meaning of the word. Readers can use them to help figure out the meaning of a word.

Alvin was <u>disqualified</u> from the race because he pushed another runner. His team then lost the track meet.

13 **In this paragraph, the word <u>disqualified</u> means —**

   A punished.

   B not eligible.

   C given another chance.

   D given a head start.

Hint: The prefix "dis-" means lack *or* opposite of.

Mr. Bozzone told his class they must read the <u>preface</u> of the book. It has important information in it.

14 **In this paragraph, the word <u>preface</u> means —**

   F bibliography.

   G introduction.

   H glossary.

   J cover.

Hint: The prefix "pre-" means before.

Justine and Marta are excited about the <u>expansion</u> of the mall. They enjoy shopping together.

15 **What does the word <u>expansion</u> mean in this sentence?**

   A modernization

   B redesign

   C enlargement

   D transfer of ownership

Hint: The suffix "-ion" means the act of doing something.

Objective 2: Identifying Theme and Story Elements

The setting is the when and where of a story. The characters are the people or people-like figures in the story. The plot is the sequence of events that makes up the core of the story.

Mark, Kim, and Jana walked cautiously up the porch steps. Marc pushed the door until it opened slowly. Jana knew they shouldn't go in the house, but their curiosity got the best of them. Inside, there loomed a shadowy hallway with towering ceilings and four doorways leading to vacant rooms. Mark and Jana stopped to stare at the parlor, while Kim bravely went into the next room. All of a sudden, Jana heard a loud crash from the adjacent room that sounded like a board breaking. Suddenly, Kim yelled, "Help me! My foot smashed through the floor, and I'm stuck."

Mark and Jana ran to help Kim. She was in the middle of the room desperately holding on to an old chair, with her foot caught in the floor. "Don't come near me," she cried. "I'm surrounded by rotten floor boards, and I'm afraid the entire floor will collapse if you try to walk on it."

"I remember seeing some pieces of lumber on the side of the porch," Jana said. "If we lay them across the floor, we can probably crawl along the boards until we reach you."

Mark rushed out and got the boards while Jana consoled Kim, who was crying. Soon, Mark came back, laid the boards on top of the old floor, and helped Kim get free. After this incident they left, and they all vowed never to go into that house again.

1 **What problem had to be solved in order to rescue Kim?**

A How to get Kim to the hall

B How to keep Kim calm

C How to keep Kim from falling through the floor

D How to get Kim back home

Hint: Read the entire passage.

2 **What is the overall mood that the author establishes in this passage?**

F joyous

G bored

H belligerent

J tense

Hint: Think about the words used to describe the setting.

For the first fifteen minutes, all Holly and Della saw were fish swimming in and out of the beams of light from their flashlights. Then Della noticed a slightly elongated rise on the ocean floor, almost like a giant oval. It seemed about fifty yards long. When Della signaled to Holly that she had found something, she swam over to see what it was. It seems that they had uncovered some kind of a ship.

3 **From the information in the paragraph, you can conclude that —**

A Holly and Della were fishing.

B Holly and Della were scuba diving.

C Holly and Della were afraid of the ocean.

D Holly and Della were on vacation.

Hint: Read the entire paragraph. Picture the scene in your mind.

No part of this document may be reproduced without permission of publisher.

Answers

1 Ⓐ Ⓑ Ⓒ Ⓓ   3 Ⓐ Ⓑ Ⓒ Ⓓ

2 Ⓕ Ⓖ Ⓗ Ⓙ

STOP

Objective 2: Drawing Conclusions

A good reader will analyze what he or she reads and make his or her own judgment about the text. Often, things are implied in a text, rather than stated directly.

Henry Hudson was an explorer for the Dutch East India Company in England, and made many trips to North America. During his last trip in 1610, he founded what is now Hudson Bay. Though some crewmen liked Hudson, others did not. Hudson, his son, and seven loyal crew members were left behind at Hudson Bay.

4   Why do you think Hudson and his men were left behind?

    F   Hudson wanted to live there.

    G   The rest of the crew started a mutiny.

    H   Hudson did not want to return to England.

    J   Hudson wanted to keep exploring.

Hint: What does the third sentence imply?

Coach Stillman said, "Girls, I'm so proud of you. I know I've never seen you play this well," as he gave the basketball team a pep talk. "You worked together, displayed all the tactics you had practiced, and made me feel truly honored to be your coach." He also said, "Remember, how you play the game is the most important thing, and this was the best played game I've seen in a long time."

5   From Coach Stillman's words, you can conclude that

    A   the girls won because they played a good game.

    B   Coach Stillman is angry.

    C   the girls lost even though they played a good game.

    D   the players are happy because they played a good game.

Hint: None of the choices are stated in the paragraph, but one of them is a conclusion that you can make from reading the paragraph.

Legend has it that William Shakespeare began his career in the theater as an assistant. Others believe that he was an unsuccessful actor. What is known is that he was recognized as a playwright and actor by 1592. His world-famous works include *Romeo and Juliet* and *Macbeth*.

6   What does the information in the paragraph imply?

    F   Nobody really knows how Shakespeare's career began.

    G   Shakespeare acted in *Macbeth*.

    H   Shakespeare went to acting school.

    J   Shakespeare went to playwriting school.

Hint: What do the first two sentences imply?

Answers

4 Ⓕ Ⓖ Ⓗ Ⓙ   6 Ⓕ Ⓖ Ⓗ Ⓙ

s20   5 Ⓐ Ⓑ Ⓒ Ⓓ

Objective 2: Drawing Conclusions

When a reader makes an inference, it means that the information in the passage has told the reader something indirectly.

Lyme disease is currently the most common tick-spread disease in North America. It has become more widespread since it was identified in Lyme, Connecticut, in the early 1970s. Today, it is found all over the world and is in almost every state in the United States. People who contact Lyme disease go through several stages of the illness. During early-stage Lyme disease, a rash can appear three to 32 days after the tick bite, and can last from two to four weeks. After the initial symptoms surface, they often disappear. However, Lyme disease can lay dormant in the body for decades. If not treated in the early stage, a person can develop late-stage Lyme, which can be quite serious.

7 After reading this paragraph, you may conclude that —

A after the rash disappears, it is certain that the disease will go away.

B people may believe they are cured once the rash disappears, but often, they are not.

C late-stage Lyme disease cannot be prevented.

D if a rash doesn't appear within 32 days after being bit by a tick, you have late-stage Lyme disease.

Hint: Look for the choice that is not written in the passage, but implied.

While on their way home from school, Kendra and Ling came upon what looked like a jewelry box. It was a beautifully carved wooden box. They wondered who would leave something like this out in the open, so they decided to investigate. When they opened the box, they found the contents to be a diamond ring, two gold necklaces, and a pair of sapphire earrings. Kendra and Ling adored the jewelry, but knew that the person who lost it must be very upset. Therefore, they took the box to the police. The owner of the jewelry was found and the police told her what had happened.

8 What do you think happened after the owner was found?

F She accused the girls of stealing the jewelry.

G She let the girls keep the jewelry.

H She sold the jewelry and gave them reward money.

J She gave them each a $50 reward.

Hint: Which answer is the most reasonable?

9 What can you conclude about the character of the two girls?

A They were selfish.

B They were honest.

C They were frightened.

D They were careless.

Hint: Kendra and Ling's actions in the story tell you something about them.

No part of this document may be reproduced without permission of publisher.

Answers

7 Ⓐ Ⓑ Ⓒ Ⓓ   9 Ⓐ Ⓑ Ⓒ Ⓓ

8 Ⓕ Ⓖ Ⓗ Ⓙ

STOP

Objective 2: Inferring Relationships

Often when we read, we need to see cause-and-effect relationships. Knowing what happened and what made it happen will help us to better understand what we read.

Animals are an important part of the continent of Africa. Each separate region has its own unique inhabitants. Deserts are home to snakes and camels. Grasslands, or savannahs, are filled with zebras, giraffes, elephants, and lions. Monkeys, parrots, and leopards live in the tropical rain forests. Even though they are significant to African life, many of them are becoming endangered species due to poachers. In order to save the existing animals, the governments of many countries have created wildlife sanctuaries to protect them.

10 **Why are wildlife sanctuaries built?**

    F So African animals will always have food

    G So tourists can see a wide variety of African animals

    H To protect animals from becoming endangered

    J They are significant to African life

Hint: Read the entire passage.

11 **What is likely to happen now that the animals are in sanctuaries?**

    A Only species from the tropical areas will be safe.

    B Species from all areas will grow in numbers.

    C Poachers will continue to kill the animals.

    D The sanctuary will be turned into a zoo.

Hint: What do you think will happen to the animals once they are saved from the poachers?

There are many reasons why you should not smoke. The primary reason is that smoking causes damage to the respiratory system. This can lead to life-threatening diseases such as emphysema and lung cancer. It lowers your quality of life, shortens your life span, and can eventually lead to an early death. Your family and friends' lives are at risk as well due to the second-hand smoke they inhale. The secondary reasons for not smoking are that your clothes, car, and house will smell dingy and dirty. Also, smoking wastes money since cigarettes are expensive. Even more expensive are the doctor bills you will have to pay after getting sick because you smoke.

12 **What is NOT included as a reason you should not smoke?**

    F financial cost

    G quality of life

    H unattractive appearance

    J bad smell

Hint: Smoking is the cause. What are the effects of smoking?

Answers

10 Ⓕ Ⓖ Ⓗ Ⓙ   **12** Ⓕ Ⓖ Ⓗ Ⓙ

11 Ⓐ Ⓑ Ⓒ Ⓓ

Objective 3: Making Predictions

Often the reader can predict, or tell in advance, what is probably going to happen next. The reader must think about what would make sense if the story were to continue.

Vicki admired her sister's gold necklace. One night, she decided she would wear it without her sister's permission. She dropped it into her purse and said she would put it on when she got to her friend's house. Later, she remembered the necklace. When she reached into her purse, it was not there.

1 **What is Vicki likely to do next?**

   A Tell her sister right away

   B Go out with her friend

   C Look through the contents of her purse more carefully

   D Borrow money from her friend to replace the necklace

Hint: Think about what you would do first if you were Vicki?

José always left his skateboard in the garage. More than once he left it behind his father's car, even though his dad pointed out what could happen when he did this. One morning, as his dad was going to visit a friend, José heard a screeching noise coming from the garage.

2 **What will probably happen next in the passage?**

   F José will walk to school.

   G José will run outside and check for his skateboard.

   H José will remember to store his skateboard somewhere else.

   J José will buy a new skateboard.

Hint: Based on what you read, what seems most likely to happen next?

Kyle was being pressured by his friends to steal candy from the candy store, because they didn't have any money. He didn't want to do it, because he knew it was against the law. At the store, his friends waited outside and saw him holding three chocolate bars in his hand.

3 **What do you think Kyle will do next in the passage?**

   A He will put the candy bars back on the shelf.

   B He will eat them right away.

   C He will take the candy bars.

   D He will ask his friends to steal the candy.

Hint: Based on what the passage tells you about Kyle, what do you think he will do?

Aliah loves to cook, so she invited some friends over for dinner. She was making pasta when the telephone rang. She went into the living room and was on the phone for forty-five minutes before she remembered that dinner was cooking.

4 **What might happen next?**

   F Aliah would stop talking and serve dinner quickly.

   G Aliah would throw out the ruined pasta.

   H Aliah would continue talking to her friend.

   J Aliah would drop the phone and rush to the kitchen.

Hint: Look at the last sentences and decide what will most likely happen next.

Answers

1 Ⓐ Ⓑ Ⓒ Ⓓ   3 Ⓐ Ⓑ Ⓒ Ⓓ

2 Ⓕ Ⓖ Ⓗ Ⓙ   4 Ⓕ Ⓖ Ⓗ Ⓙ

Objective 3: Judging Author Purpose, Point of View, and Effectiveness

The author's point of view is what he or she feels about what he or she is writing. Opinions express points of view.

The only way to make our environment more livable is to reduce the use of automobiles during peak traffic hours. With so many people traveling during the same hours, we are creating a serious health problem—increasing air pollution.

The automobile is a major cause of the poor air quality. The exhaust from cars:

- depletes the earth's protective ozone layer and contributes to global warming.
- produces as much as 50% of the smog-producing compounds and acid rain in our atmosphere.
- contributes more than 60% of the carbon monoxide to our atmosphere.

The last two statistics are the most alarming of all. These pollutants are in the air that we all breathe. If our goal is to achieve clean air in the 21st century, we need to discourage car use whenever possible, especially during peak commuting hours.

Many industrialized countries have tried to reduce air pollution by controlling the emission from motor vehicles. The United States has spent billions of dollars in an effort to reduce motor vehicle pollutants. Legislation requiring automobile manufacturers to reduce exhaust emissions is in effect in the United States, yet heavily populated areas are still in violation of the public health standards for clean air.

5 According to the author —

A the use of automobiles is a necessity.

B clean air is only possible if we reduce car use during peak traffic hours.

C the United States needs to spend more money to reduce motor vehicle pollutants.

D exhaust contributes more than 50 percent of carbon monoxide to our atmosphere.

Hint: Read the entire passage.

6 What is the author's opinion of legislation concerning automobile emissions?

F Legislation has been successful in reducing air pollution.

G Legislation is able to uphold public health standards for air quality.

H Populated areas are polluted in spite of legislation.

J We need tougher anti-pollution legislation.

Hint: Read the passage and look for the author's point of view.

Graffiti on the walls and streets of our town is ugly and offensive, and people are right to want to put a stop to it. But the law stopping the sale of spray paint to minors is wrong because it punishes the wrong people. This paint law punishes the owners of stores for what customers do with spray paint. Furthermore, such a law suggests that all minors are criminals.

Before we can stop graffiti, we must understand the teen culture. Some kids write because they have something they want to say. Others write so people will notice them. This desire to be noticed is so strong it will take more than a law to stop it. We should spend more time understanding teens than passing paint laws.

7 The author feels that—

A teens should be arrested for doing graffiti.

B all teens who buy spray paint are criminals.

C adults should spend time understanding teens.

D store owners should welcome the paint law.

Hint: Think about what the author says about teens.

Answers

5 Ⓐ Ⓑ Ⓒ Ⓓ   7 Ⓐ Ⓑ Ⓒ Ⓓ

6 Ⓕ Ⓖ Ⓗ Ⓙ

STOP

Objective 4: Summarizing Content

The main idea is the overall meaning of a piece of writing. Often the main idea is written in the passage.

Albanian-born Sister Teresa first arrived in India in 1929. She was overwhelmed by all the poverty and suffering around her. She watched India struggle with foreign and domestic problems that brought increased suffering to the poor. One day, as she traveled from Calcutta to a rural area of India, Sister Teresa had a vision. She realized that her mission was to go into the worst slums of Calcutta and help India's poorest citizens. The date was September 10, 1946. The Missionaries of Charity began soon after, in 1950. A spiritual leader of this group, Sister Teresa soon became known as Mother Teresa. She was awarded the esteemed Nobel Peace Prize in 1979.

1 **What is the main idea of this paragraph?**

A Mother Teresa was awarded the Nobel Peace Prize.

B Mother Teresa traveled throughout India.

C Mother Teresa devoted her life to loving and helping people.

D Mother Teresa watched India struggle with foreign and domestic problems.

Hint: The main idea is mentioned in the middle of the paragraph.

There are several things to know when it comes to growing and maintaining your lawn. One important piece of information is knowing that all grass seed is not alike. Grasses differ in texture and rate of growth. The texture of a grass has to do with the type of leaf on the grass stem. Fine-leaf grasses have narrow blades. This grass makes evenly textured, neat lawns. They grow at a constant rate. Broad-leaf grass has a much wider blade and has a tough base. It results in a coarse-textured lawn that is difficult to mow.

2 **What does this paragraph mainly talk about?**

F Fine-leaf grasses have narrow blades.

G Grasses differ in texture and rate of growth.

H Coarse-textured lawns are difficult to mow.

J Broad-leaf grasses have a tough base.

Hint: Read the beginning of the paragraph.

While many people think about "the big picture" of our world and our universe, there are scientists who focus on small things. These scientists study microtechnology. Microtechnology involves working with and creating things that are miniature in size, such as miniature robots and tiny motors that size of a speck of dust. Also being made are microscopic sensors that can be used for exploring space, studying ecological issues, and handling materials that are hazardous. This technology is also used by auto makers for mapping systems. These systems help you by finding a car's exact location and giving you directions to your destination.

3 **What is the best summary of this paragraph?**

A Miniature inventions are less exciting than "big picture" technology.

B Scientists are developing important creations in microtechnology.

C Automobile manufacturers are producing global positioning systems.

D Some motors are no larger than a speck of dust.

Hint: Again, the main idea is mentioned at the beginning of the paragraph.

Answers

1 Ⓐ Ⓑ Ⓒ Ⓓ   **3** Ⓐ Ⓑ Ⓒ Ⓓ

2 Ⓕ Ⓖ Ⓗ Ⓙ

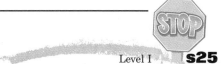

Objective 4: Using Graphics and Text Structure

Often texts come with graphics or diagrams. These are there to help the reader better understand the passage.

The Spread of the Black Death

North Sea

KEY

• 1347	≡ 1350
‖‖ 1348	○ 1351
∷ 1349	

Dublin

Hamburg
London • Cologne
Atlantic Ocean
• Paris

Genoa • Venice
Barcelona • Marseille
Rome

Black Sea • Caffo

Constantinople

Mediterranean Sea

Messina

The Black Death struck Europe during the Middle Ages, in the fourteenth century. Before the plague ran its course, it had killed more than one quarter of the population. It was the most deadly epidemic of bubonic and pneumonic plague ever recorded. It spread throughout most of Europe between 1347 and 1351.

The origins of the Black Death are not clear. Most historians think it came from southern Russia and Middle Eastern ports. From these areas it spread along trade routes including, Messina, Marseille, and Genoa. Ships carried infected rats and people from port to port. From these beginnings, the plague spread rapidly into southern France, Spain, Italy, and Greece. By 1350 it had made its way through all of France, Ireland, and much of Europe. By 1351 the Black Plague had run its course. Cases still appeared in Europe for more than 200 years; however, these were not as widespread as before. Even today, some cases of the plague will occur. But treatment is given quickly and the disease is contained.

4 Which statement is correct based on the map?

F The plague never reached Dublin.

G The plague was in Messina before Barcelona.

H The plague was in Hamburg after Paris.

J The plague moved from north to south.

Hint: Use the key to answer the question.

5 Messina and Marseille were the first two areas to be infected by the plague because —

A the first European outbreak of the plague was only in southern cities

B they were port cities vulnerable to infected rats on ships

C England and Ireland were separated from the continent

D they were cities that had larger populations

Hint: Read the passage and review the map.

Answers

4 Ⓕ Ⓖ Ⓗ Ⓙ

5 Ⓐ Ⓑ Ⓒ Ⓓ

Unit 1: Reading

    Lesson 1: Reading Comprehension..4

    Unit 1 Test..9

Unit 2: Language Arts

    Lesson 2: Sentence Structure 13

    Lesson 3: Writing Strategies 15

    Lesson 4: Editing Skills 17

    Unit 2 Test..19

Comprehensive Test: Reading and Language Arts 23

    Part 1 25

    Part 2 39

Student Answer Sheet..63

·········· **Lesson 1: Reading Comprehension**

Directions: Read each passage carefully. Then read each question. Darken the circle for the correct answer.

 Read the paragraph. Before you answer the question, think about the title of the passage. The title can help you focus on an important idea.

Sample A   **A Race Against Time**

Several plants from the Amazon rain forest have become the basis of medicines used by Western doctors. Ethnobotanists, scientists who study how plants are used in a culture, hope to learn from indigenous peoples of the Amazon about other useful plants. However, they cannot carry out their work in a leisurely fashion. Some people predict that, given the current rate of destruction, within the next fifty years most of the rain forest will be gone.

What is the main idea of this passage?

A Scientists who study how plants are used in a culture are called ethnobotanists.

B Western medicine has benefited from the discoveries of valuable plants in the Amazon rain forest.

C Ethnobotanists have a limited time in which to work with indigenous peoples of the Amazon to discover useful plants.

D It is quite probable that within the next fifty years most of the Amazon rain forest will have been destroyed.

 The correct answer is <u>C, Ethnobotanists have a limited time in which to work with indigenous peoples of the Amazon to discover useful plants</u>. The title, "A Race Against Time," tells you what aspect of the topic was important to the author.

 When you are asked about a word in a passage, find that word. Reread the sentence it appears in and look for clues to the word's meaning in nearby sentences.

Sample B   **Anchovies**

You may like to eat anchovies on a pizza, or maybe you know someone who does. What *is* an anchovy? Actually, the name is applied to any of several small, bony fishes. They're all related to the herring. Most species are less than six inches long, but the largest reaches lengths of up to twenty inches. Anchovies are common in the open waters of tropical climates. However, in the recent past the anchovy population off the coasts of Chile and Peru has been seriously depleted, mostly because of overfishing and the climatic disturbances of El Niño.

What does the word *depleted* mean?

F disturbed   **H** destroyed

G eliminated   **J** reduced

 The correct answer is <u>J, reduced</u>. The word *overfishing* and the phrase *climatic disturbances of El Niño* provide clues to the meaning of *depleted*. Also, the previous sentence tells you that anchovies are common. The next sentence begins with the word *however*, setting up a contrast that will help you to infer the word's meaning.

Answers
SA Ⓐ Ⓑ ● Ⓓ
4 SB Ⓕ Ⓖ Ⓗ ●

Directions: Read the first part of this article about a special camp in Maine where Israeli and Palestinian teenagers learn to live together. Then read each question. Darken the circle for the correct answer.

Cameras Help Teenagers Look Beyond Bitter Conflicts
by Joel Greenberg

Amer Kamal, a seventeen-year-old Palestinian from East Jerusalem, looks squarely into the video camera and addresses his Israeli friend, Yaron Avni, eighteen, who will soon be drafted into the Israeli army:

"I hope that you will be a good soldier who helps his society, who helps his people, and who works for the peace process. I don't want to see you . . . running after Palestinians and killing them. I hope you're going to stay the Yaron I know." Yaron says his Palestinian friend has no cause for alarm. "I can assure Amer that I will always stay humane," he says. "That's how I was brought up."

In the Middle East, where Israelis and Palestinians have been fighting each other for generations, an exchange like this one is rare. Amer and Yaron are part of a team that filmed *Peace of Mind*, the first documentary ever shot jointly by Israeli and Palestinian youths, chronicling a year in their lives after returning home from an Israeli-Arab summer camp in the Maine woods.

The camp is run by Seeds of Peace, one of the best-known organizations promoting reconciliation between Arab and Israeli youth. Founded in 1993, the organization has won praise for bringing together Israeli, Palestinian, and other Arab teenagers for three-and-a-half-week sessions to build friendships and discuss ways to resolve the conflict between their peoples.

"But what happens when they go back home?" asks Susan Siegel, co-executive director of Global Action Project, an educational group that produced the film. "That's the real story."

To find out, Siegel and director Mark Landsman chose four Israelis and three Palestinians, trained them in the use of video cameras, and asked them to document their lives starting in the summer of 1997. The teenagers shot 175 hours of tape and met periodically to review the footage and outline the film, testing their ability to work together and to portray some of the most wrenching issues of the Israeli-Palestinian conflict.

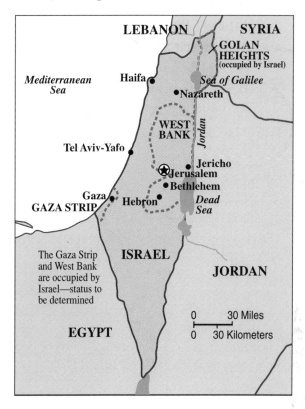

1   **What is the subject of the film *Peace of Mind*?**

   A   the lives of Israeli and Palestinian youths at a camp in Maine

   B   the Israeli-Palestinian conflict and its effects on young people

   C   the lives of Israeli and Palestinian youths in their homeland

   D   the difficulty of forming friendships among Israeli and Palestinian youths

2   **How did production of the documentary relate to the youths' experience at the summer camp?**

   F   At the camp they were taught video production skills to use once they arrived home.

   G   The trust and cooperation that had developed among them at the camp was put to the test while creating the documentary.

   H   They were told at the camp to make a documentary about their interaction once they were back in their own environments.

   J   While at the camp, they planned the documentary they would shoot after returning to their homelands.

3   **What does the word *reconciliation* mean in the fourth paragraph?**

   A   a search for compromise

   B   the act of praising

   C   the formation of a relationship

   D   a settling of a dispute

4   **Which of these phrases does <u>not</u> support your answer for Number 3?**

   F   has won praise

   G   for bringing together

   H   resolve the conflict

   J   build friendships

Answers

  1   Ⓐ Ⓑ Ⓒ Ⓓ   **3**   Ⓐ Ⓑ Ⓒ Ⓓ

  2   Ⓕ Ⓖ Ⓗ Ⓙ   **4**   Ⓕ Ⓖ Ⓗ Ⓙ

Directions: Read the conclusion of "Cameras Help Teenagers Look Beyond Bitter Conflicts," by Joel Greenberg. Then read each question. Darken the circle for the correct answer.

At one point, an emotional argument about terrorism nearly broke up the group and threatened to end the project. Yossi Zilberman, eighteen, an Israeli, called bombers from the militant Islamic group Hamas "animals." Amer argued that although the militants were wrong, they were patriots who had sacrificed their lives for their country.

The debate ended in tears. "It was scary to hear your friend talking like that," says Sivan Ranon, a seventeen-year-old Israeli. "Suddenly you felt that you don't know this person."

The teens also argued over history. Each side has an opposing narrative of the same events. When Israel was created in 1948, for instance, were the Palestinians expelled from their land, or did they flee a war started by Arab states bent on destroying Israel? "The differences between my history and your history are huge," says Yaron, speaking into a camera held by Amer. "It's not even close. We say one thing and you say the opposite. You say one thing and we totally disagree."

The film deals with the dispute by including two separate sequences, one in which the Palestinians show the displacement of their people in the 1948 Arab-Israeli war, and another in which the Israelis tell of a Jewish return to an ancient homeland in the wake of the Holocaust.

There were also concerns on both sides about the Israelis' impending army service, which is compulsory after high school. "What if they ask me to go and be in a base in the West Bank or East Jerusalem?" Reut Elkoubi, a seventeen-year-old Israeli, asks in the film. "I have friends over there. God, Amer lives in East Jerusalem."

Bushra Jawabri, an eighteen-year-old Palestinian, formed a close friendship with Sivan, exchanging home visits they documented in the film. But Bushra is concerned about what her Israeli friend might do when she puts on a uniform. "Although I trust her that she really wants coexistence, what if her government asks her to do something against the other side?" Bushra says. "You never know. I don't want to see Sivan carrying a gun in front of me, and me carrying a stone against her."

Sivan, for her part, says that no matter how close she is to Bushra, her friend's dream of returning to her refugee family's native village inside Israel remains a barrier between them. "She represents a whole population that wants to come back and live in our place, and that's scary," Sivan says. "Her dream is my nightmare. Although we're best friends, I'll never be able to help make her dream come true."

Now that the film is finished (it has already been shown in Israel and will be shown in several locations in the United States), both sides have reservations about Landsman's final editing. Yossi and Yaron criticize portrayals that they consider unfair to the Israelis, while Amer and Palestinian teenager Hazem Zaanoun complain that the film lacks a broader range of Palestinian views.

But no one expected the video would bring an end to fifty years of bloody conflict. "We got to know each other, for better and for worse," Yossi says. "I'm still for peace, but I'm much more realistic. I know what I'm up against. I'm more sober. We're all more sober."

But if serious differences remain, the film also captures the teenagers forging human connections across the ethnic divide. "If I'm talking about Palestinians, I'm not talking about Palestinians only because I've heard about them," Sivan says in the film. "I know people from the other side, and they're not monsters, they're people, like us."

Moments like these, the producers hope, may be the region's real seeds of peace.

5 Which of these best describes the tone of this passage?

A opinionated

B tense

C informative

D pessimistic

6 What does the author say may be the real "seeds of peace" in the Middle East?

F instances in which Israeli and Palestinian teenagers make connections despite their differences

G Israeli and Palestinian teenagers' acknowledgment of how difficult it will be to resolve the Middle East conflict

H changes in Israeli and Palestinian teenagers' views toward being more realistic about the situation in the Middle East

J the sessions in which Israeli and Palestinian teenagers had to work together to create the documentary

7 The author says that both sides have *reservations* about the final editing of the film. The word *reservations* probably means

A disagreements about a subject

B arrangements to set aside and hold something

C lands set aside for special use

D doubts that limit an acceptance of something

8 What is the most probable purpose the author had in mind when he wrote this article?

F to analyze the effects of a documentary production on a group of Palestinian and Israeli youths

G to publicize a documentary filmed by Palestinian and Israeli youths after they lived together in a summer camp

H to describe a summer camp in Maine where Palestinian and Israeli youths are encouraged to forge human connections despite their historical disputes

J to describe the complex relationships that develop between Palestinian and Israeli youths brought together under special circumstances

9 What is the most probable reason that the documentary includes one sequence of the displacement of Palestinians in the 1948 Arab-Israeli war and another of Jews returning to an ancient homeland after the Holocaust?

A to illustrate the drastic difference in perspectives held by the Palestinian and Israeli youths

B to avoid alienating either Jewish or Palestinian audiences

C to provide the viewer with the historical background of the Palestinian and Israeli youths featured in the documentary

D to encourage an equal number of Palestinian and Israeli youths to attend the Seeds of Peace camp in the future

Directions: Read the passage carefully. Then read the question. Darken the circle for the correct answer.

Sample

Virtual Gorilla

The Virtual Reality Gorilla Exhibit at the Atlanta, Georgia, zoo shows you what it is like to be a gorilla. You don a virtual reality helmet and suddenly you are in a naturalistic setting inhabited by gorillas. During the simulation, you interact with the gorillas and communicate by making body postures, gestures, facial expressions, and sounds like those of a gorilla.

What does *don* mean in this passage?

A check out

B manipulate

C put on

D examine

Directions: Here is an article about the coldest continent on our planet. Read the article carefully. Darken the circle for the correct answer.

About Antarctica

Learn the cold, hard truth about this land of extremes.

Antarctica is the coldest, windiest, highest, and driest continent on Earth! About the size of the United States and Mexico combined, Antarctica is actually a desert 98% covered by a thick ice sheet. This sheet of ice is by far the largest body of fresh water and of ice on Earth, comprising nearly 70% of the whole world's total of fresh water. The weight of all this ice pushes Antarctica below sea level.

Huge ice shelves extend outward from about half of Antarctica's coastline. These ice shelves melt from December to March, during which the temperature can rise to 0° Fahrenheit. That's pretty comfortable for Antarctica. The ice shelves form June to September, when the temperature drops to −65° Fahrenheit. During the winter months, the size of the ice shelves nearly doubles the area of the continent.

Most supplies arrive just once a year on a container ship called the *Green Wave*. This ship then hauls out trash and waste collected during the year. Everyone on the continent is extra careful about recycling so that the beauty of Antarctica is preserved.

It's so cold in the Antarctic seas and along the coast that penguins, fish, whales, and seals are among the few animals that can survive the frigid temperatures. Once a year, emperor penguins return from the sea to the coast and spend about thirty-four days shedding their feather coats and growing new ones. This is called molting. The new feathers keep them warm in the winter.

Two natural hazards cause big problems in Antarctica: katabatic winds and the ozone hole. Katabatic winds blow toward the coast from the high interior of the continent. The winds can reach hurricane

---

Answers

S Ⓐ Ⓑ Ⓒ Ⓓ

strength and cause blizzards. Ozone, a gas that occurs naturally in the upper atmosphere, normally blocks harmful solar radiation. But there's a region of the upper atmosphere where the amount of ozone is below average. The "hole" creates problems in the Antarctic ecosystem. For example, research shows that radiation (normally blocked by the ozone layer) has damaged the DNA of some Antarctic fish.

Summertime in Antarctica (December to March) means twenty-four hours of daylight, and winter (June to September) means twenty-four hours of darkness. At the South Pole, the first sunset of the year 2000 took place on February 21. After that date, the amount of daylight decreased eighteen minutes a day until it was completely dark for twenty-four hours. The sun didn't rise again until September 10, so if you're planning a visit, check the dates before you pack your sunglasses.

Cool Facts About Antarctica

- From the end of February until late August, no planes fly to or from Antarctica. During this time, satellite-relayed phone calls and e-mail provide the only links with the outside world.

- McMurdo Station is the largest research station on the continent. Up to 1,100 people live and work there during the summer. Only about 200 live there during the winter. The South Pole station has about 200 residents in the summer and about 40 in the winter.

- Less than two inches of rain falls in the interior of Antarctica each year, making it drier than the Sahara.

- In 1961, more than forty nations ratified the Antarctic Treaty, which set aside and preserved Antarctica for peaceful scientific use only.

---

1 **In July, the area of Antarctica is almost twice the size it is in February because of**

A fewer hours of daylight

B the ice shelves that form along part of the coastline

C blizzards in the continent's interior

D the thick ice sheet that covers 98% of the continent

2 **According to the article, why is recycling so important in Antarctica?**

F Recycling trash and waste is easier than burning it in the cold temperatures.

G Recycling helps reduce the amount of trash the *Green Wave* must haul out.

H People do not want the wildlife living off humans' trash and waste.

J Recycling reduces the amount of trash that might diminish the continent's beauty.

3 **With regard to summer and winter in Antarctica, which of these is <u>not</u> compared in the article?**

A hours of daylight

B extent of the ice shelves off the coastline

C intensity of the katabatic winds

D number of people living there

4 **Which of these conclusions can you draw from the article?**

F Emperor penguins migrate to Antarctica in June each year.

G The area of Antarctica is greater than that of the United States.

H Research scientists prefer to work in Antarctica during the winter.

J McMurdo Station has more people in the summer because of the katabatic winds.

Answers

1 Ⓐ Ⓑ Ⓒ Ⓓ   3 Ⓐ Ⓑ Ⓒ Ⓓ

10 2 Ⓕ Ⓖ Ⓗ Ⓙ   4 Ⓕ Ⓖ Ⓗ Ⓙ

Directions: Here is an interview with Sandra Markle, a correspondent who spent time in Antarctica.

A Look Back at Antarctica

Time for Kids' South Pole reporter reflects on life at the bottom of the world.

TFK: How do you feel now that you've left Antarctica? Do you feel there are other parts of this polar region you'd like to explore?

Markle: Spending the winter in Antarctica was a wonderful adventure. Antarctica, though, is bigger than the United States and Mexico combined. I'd still like to join one of the expeditions to the top of Mount Erebus, one of the active volcanoes in Antarctica. Imagine seeing molten lava in the midst of all that ice!

TFK: Did your experience over the past six months differ from your first expectations of Antarctica?

Markle: My winter in Antarctica was even more amazing than I'd anticipated. First, I had a chance to see the Adelie penguins go through their annual molt, replacing old feathers with a new coat. The sunset was spectacular and lasted for weeks, since the sun was visible twenty-four hours a day until it slipped below the horizon. Once the five-month-long night started, the sky became a screen of auroras—dancing curtains of fluorescent green light. Even the storms were awesome. Sometimes the wind gusts would push me backward, and the blowing snow made everything a white blur. And the cold was incredible—with wind chills as cold as −109° Fahrenheit.

TFK: Twenty years from now, what do you think you'll remember most about your experience?

Markle: I know I'll remember the dramatic weather. Surviving such extreme cold and fierce storms let me know that I'm strong enough to face any challenge. I will also remember the special friends I made in Antarctica. From February through August, the two hundred two of us only had each other to keep water flowing, to keep electricity generating, and to stay safe throughout the coldest, fiercest winter on Earth.

TFK: During bad weather, what was the best way to pass the time?

Markle: I took along watercolors and painted pictures. I also read mysteries and books written about Antarctica by early explorers. It was interesting to read about their struggles to survive Antarctica's harsh conditions. By comparison, I had it really easy. What I enjoyed most were the dorm gatherings. Lots of people would get together in the building's lounge. We'd share snacks, talk, and play games like Balderdash.

TFK: What are some activities that are popular in Antarctica but would never catch on in America?

Markle: In Antarctica, people recycle everything. I can't imagine anyone back home in the United States getting excited about scavenging through piles of stuff for half-empty jars of jelly or leftover coffee. It was also a fad to dress entirely in skuaed clothes. Finding something you can reuse is called skuaing—named for the skua bird that's Antarctica's skilled scavenger. I never pictured myself putting together outfits from old clothes and shoes, but I did.

TFK: If you were given a million dollars to make life in Antarctica more comfortable, what would you spend it on?

Markle: I'd enlarge the greenhouse. The current one is about the size of a minivan. Using hydroponics and artificial lighting, it supplies the community with a taste of fresh lettuce about once a month. It's also great to see green growing plants when it's dark and super cold outdoors.

TFK: If you could be any animal in Antarctica, what would you be?

Markle: I'd want to be a killer whale. They're at the top of the food chain. They are majestic to see up close in the wild. During one of my two summers in Antarctica, I had a chance to fly by helicopter out to the ice edge. I was just a few feet away from the water, taking pictures of penguins, when a pod, or a group, of killer whales popped their heads up to check me out. It was amazing to be eye-to-eye with a killer whale.

On second thought, I'd rather be a skua, because then I could fly north when it gets too cold!

TFK: What do you think is the biggest misconception people have about Antarctica?

Markle: The one thing that seems to surprise people about the polar regions is that there are no polar bears in Antarctica and no penguins in the Arctic. People also have no idea of how cold it really is during the Antarctic winter. There are no words that can describe what −109° Fahrenheit feels like. It's intense and painful. I could never pop outdoors for even a second without first putting on my ECW (Extreme Cold Weather) gear—about 40 pounds of clothing.

---

5 Which of these statements by Sandra Markle is a *fact*?

 A Sometimes the wind gusts would push me backwards, and the blowing snow made everything a white blur.

 B My winter in Antarctica was even more amazing than I'd anticipated.

 C It was interesting to read about their [early explorers'] struggles to survive Antarctica's harsh conditions.

 D On second thought, I'd rather be a skua, because then I could fly north when it gets too cold!

6 What is the best synonym for the word *scavenging*?

 F looking

 G separating

 H sifting

 J rummaging

7 The interviewer was probably most interested in

 A Sandra Markle's future adventures

 B the difficult living conditions in Antarctica

 C the weather in Antarctica

 D Sandra Markle's experiences in Antarctica

8 Which of these is least likely to be true about Sandra Markle?

 F She is willing to take risks.

 G She knows how to entertain herself.

 H She wants to make a million dollars.

 J She will miss the friends she made at McMurdo.

9 The interview with Sandra Markle could best be used to document

 A basic facts about killer whales

 B day-to-day living in Antarctica

 C surviving the coldest, fiercest winter on Earth

 D misconceptions Americans have about living in Antarctica

10 To select the answer for Number 9, which of these would be the most appropriate strategy?

 F look for the title of the passage

 G review the passage to find quotations

 H outline the passage and detail each step

 J reread the interviewer's questions

Answers

5 Ⓐ Ⓑ Ⓒ Ⓓ   **7** Ⓐ Ⓑ Ⓒ Ⓓ   **9** Ⓐ Ⓑ Ⓒ Ⓓ

12 **6** Ⓕ Ⓖ Ⓗ Ⓙ   **8** Ⓕ Ⓖ Ⓗ Ⓙ   **10** Ⓕ Ⓖ Ⓗ Ⓙ

·········· **Lesson 2: Sentence Structure**

Directions: Read each sample. Darken the circle for the correct answer.

Choose the answer that shows the best way to correct these clauses.

Sample A

When people lose their sense of smell, people usually complain. That their quality of life has been negatively affected.

A When people lose their sense of smell. People usually complain that their quality of life has been negatively affected.

B When people lose their sense of smell, people usually complain that their quality of life has been negatively affected.

C When people lose their sense of smell, they usually complain. People's quality of life has been negatively affected.

D When people lose their sense of smell, they usually complain that their quality of life has been negatively affected.

The correct answer is D, When people lose their sense of smell, they usually complain that their quality of life has been negatively affected. It is the only choice in which the clauses are correctly combined and pronouns are used correctly.

Choose the sentence that is correctly punctuated.

Sample B

Usually, people who have lost their sense of smell don't enjoy foods, also, they may sleep poorly because they fear they won't detect smoke if there's a fire.

F Usually, people who have lost their sense of smell don't enjoy foods; also, they may sleep poorly because they fear they won't detect smoke if there's a fire.

G Usually people who have lost their sense of smell don't enjoy foods, also, they may sleep poorly, because they fear they won't detect smoke, if there's a fire.

H Usually, people who have lost their sense of smell don't enjoy foods, also, they may sleep poorly; because they fear they won't detect smoke, if there's a fire.

J Usually people who have lost their sense of smell don't enjoy foods, also they may sleep poorly, because they fear they won't detect smoke if there's a fire.

The correct answer is F, Usually, people who have lost their sense of smell don't enjoy foods; also, they may sleep poorly because they fear they won't detect smoke if there's a fire. This is the only sentence in which commas and a semicolon are used correctly.

Answers
SA Ⓐ Ⓑ Ⓒ Ⓓ
SB Ⓕ Ⓖ Ⓗ Ⓙ

Directions: Choose the answer that shows the best way to correct the sentence.

1 *Mexico City, one of the older cities in the Western Hemisphere was builded on what was once a lake bed.*

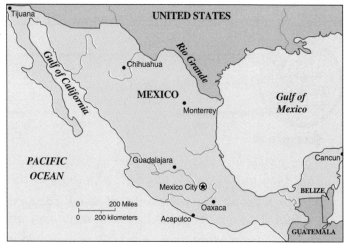

A Mexico City one of the older cities in the Western Hemisphere, was built on what was once a lake bed.

B Mexico City, one of the older cities in the western hemisphere was built on what was once a lake bed.

C Mexico City, one of the oldest cities in the Western Hemisphere, was built on what was once a lake bed.

D Mexico City, one of the oldest cities in the Western Hemisphere was builded on what was once a lake bed.

2 *Soft and spongy, Mexico City sits on soil that magnifies the shock waves of the earthquakes that shakes it regularly.*

F Soft and spongy Mexico City sits on soil that magnifies the shock waves of the earthquakes that shake it regularly.

G Soft and spongy, Mexico City sits on soil which magnifies the shock waves of the earthquakes that shake Mexico City regularly.

H Mexico City sits on soil, soft and spongy, which magnifies the shock waves of the earthquakes that shakes it regularly.

J Mexico City sits on soft and spongy soil that magnifies the shock waves of the earthquakes that shake it regularly.

Directions: Read the three sentences. Choose the sentence that most effectively combines them.

3 *An earthquake hit Mexico City in 1985. It was particularly devastating. An estimated 8,000 people were killed.*

A A particularly devastating earthquake hit Mexico City in 1985, killing an estimated 8,000 people.

B In 1985 an estimated 8,000 people in Mexico City were killed by an earthquake, particularly devastating.

C An estimated 8,000 people were devastated and killed by an earthquake in Mexico City in 1985.

D Killing an estimated 8,000 people was a particularly devastating earthquake that hit Mexico City, in 1985.

Directions: Choose the group of words that forms a complete sentence.

4 F Many buildings are sinking into the soft soil of the former lake bed.

G Some sinking as much as one foot each year.

H New building construction, which must meet government regulations.

J Height restrictions and improved types of foundations included in the regulations.

Answers

1 Ⓐ Ⓑ Ⓒ Ⓓ   **3** Ⓐ Ⓑ Ⓒ Ⓓ

14 **2** Ⓕ Ⓖ Ⓗ Ⓙ   **4** Ⓕ Ⓖ Ⓗ Ⓙ

Level I

Lesson 3: Writing Strategies

Directions: Read each sample. Darken the circle for the correct answer.

Try This

Choose the sentence that best completes the passage. First, think about the sequence of ideas in the paragraph.

Sample A

There are several methods of plant propagation. The most common, of course, is planting seeds. Some plants, however, are best propagated using other methods. Stem-cutting is one method. Softwood cuttings can be taken in late spring or early summer from plants with green, flexible stems. Some plants will form roots if you use the method called ground-layering—securely placing a lower branch in shallow soil. _____ . When you buy a plant, ask an employee which propagation method should be used.

A Hardwood cuttings are usually taken in late winter or early spring.

B Another method, called division, consists of lifting shallow-rooted plants from the soil and gently pulling them apart.

C Not all plants grow easily from seeds; many herbs fall into this category.

D Carefully follow the steps involved in the method of propagation you have decided to use.

Think It Through

The correct answer is B, <u>Another method, called division, consists of lifting shallow-rooted plants from the soil and gently pulling them apart.</u> This is the only sentence that logically fits into the sequence of ideas presented in the paragraph.

Try This

Choose the best concluding sentence for the passage. Think about which sentence best summarizes the information in the paragraph.

Sample B

Some studies of stress in animals have shown that humans aren't the only ones to get stressed out. Baboons also can experience enough stress to have their health affected. Baboons are very social creatures that live in high-stress societies. (This means that in a troop of baboons, higher-ranked baboons intimidate lower-ranked ones to maintain order.) Too much stress can cause mothers to produce unhealthy offspring. It can also damage a baboon's brain in the region called the hippocampus. _____ .

F The hippocampus plays an important role in learning and memory.

G Baboons and other animals share with humans the emotional characteristic of stress.

H So, even though baboons don't have to take algebra tests, they can suffer serious health consequences as a result of getting stressed out.

J A baboon's social behavior affects the levels of stress hormones its body produces.

Think It Through

The correct answer is H, <u>So, even though baboons don't have to take algebra tests, they can suffer serious health consequences as a result of getting stressed out.</u> This sentence makes reference to the idea in the topic sentence and summarizes much of the information in the paragraph.

Answers

SA Ⓐ Ⓑ Ⓒ Ⓓ

SB Ⓕ Ⓖ Ⓗ Ⓙ

Directions: Choose the word or phrase that best completes the paragraph.

1 *A desert is a harsh environment—so harsh that it seems unlikely that life forms could thrive in it. _____ , a desert is alive with plants and animals that have adapted to the environment. Each species has special ways of surviving the scarcity of water and the extreme temperatures.*

A Therefore

B In contrast

C As a consequence

D Nevertheless

Directions: Choose the sentence that is least relevant to the paragraph.

2 [1.] Daytime temperatures in a desert frequently reach over 100˚ Fahrenheit. [2.] Desert animals, including snakes, have adapted to such heat. [3.] Large animals are scarce in the desert, but some rodents such as desert rats are plentiful. [4.] Since the body temperature of snakes changes according to the surrounding air, desert snakes must hide in cracks and holes in the ground during the hottest parts of the day. [5.] If a snake stayed in the sun all day long, it would die because its blood would boil.

F Sentence 2   **G** Sentence 3   **H** Sentence 4   **J** Sentence 5

Directions: Choose the sentence that best fits in the blank.

3 *_____ . One desert rodent, the kangaroo rat, never takes a drink of water. Instead, it gets the water it needs from the seeds it eats. The Arabian camel gets water from thorny desert plants that it is equipped to bite off and consume. During the few rains that fall each year in the Arizona desert, the saguaro cactus expands like an accordion to take in water that it stores and later uses slowly.*

A Desert plants such as cacti must be able to survive on only tiny amounts of water.

B Seeds provide water for some desert animals.

C One reason a desert is such a harsh environment is that water is often unavailable.

D Desert plants and animals have ways of coping with the lack of water in their environment.

4 *Some woody desert plants have root systems long enough to reach deep water sources. Many desert plants have thorns, which are modified leaves, that discourage animals from eating them. The small leaves of desert plants contribute to water conservation because there is less surface area from which transpiration can occur. _____ .*

F Obviously, the root system of a desert plant is a major factor in its ability to thrive in the desert.

G The leaves of desert plants contribute to their survival in a variety of ways.

H Desert plants have special ways of obtaining and storing water.

J As you can see, the structures of desert plants contribute to their survival.

Answers

1 Ⓐ Ⓑ Ⓒ Ⓓ   3 Ⓐ Ⓑ Ⓒ Ⓓ

16 2 Ⓕ Ⓖ Ⓗ Ⓙ   4 Ⓕ Ⓖ Ⓗ Ⓙ

Level I

Directions: Read each draft. Darken the circle for the correct answer.

¹· Haiku is a Japanese verse form. ²· It consists of three unrhymed lines, the first line has five syllables, the second has seven, and the third has five. ³· Traditionally, a pair of contrasting images are presented in a haiku. ⁴· One of the images suggests time and place; the other image is an observation, subtle yet powerful. ⁵· In general, it is up to the reader to make the connection between the two images—to perceive what the poet was "painting" with his or her words. ⁶· Together the images create mood and emotion.

Which sentence contains a mistake in the use of punctuation? Read each sentence carefully.

Sample A

A Sentence 2
B Sentence 4
C Sentence 5
D None of them

The correct answer is A, Sentence 2. A semicolon instead of a comma is required after *lines*. Otherwise, a run-on sentence is created.

Which sentence contains a mistake in agreement? Read each sentence carefully.

Sample B

F Sentence 3
G Sentence 4
H Sentence 5
J None of them

The correct answer is F, Sentence 3. The sentence contains a mistake in subject-verb agreement. The subject of this sentence, *pair*, is singular. It needs a singular verb, *is*.

Answers
SA Ⓐ Ⓑ Ⓒ Ⓓ
SB Ⓕ Ⓖ Ⓗ Ⓙ

Directions: Read this draft of a paragraph about a famous children's author. Then answer the questions that follow. Darken the circle for the correct answer.

1. Theodor Seuss Geisel, known as Dr Seuss to millions of children all over the world was born in Springfield, Massachusetts in 1904. 2. While still a boy, he started drawing fantastic animals; probably influenced by the fact that his father ran the local zoo. 3. Based on the number of his books that have sold (over 80 million), he is among the popularest writers in the world. 4. He accomplished this even though one of his art teachers told him he would never learn to draw and his first children's book was rejected by 29 publishers. 5. A lesser-known fact about Geisel is that twice he won an Academy Award. 6. The first time was in 1947 for a documentary about the Japanese people; the second time was in 1951 for creating a cartoon character called Gerald McBoing Boing.

1 **Choose the best way to rewrite Sentence 1.**

A Theodor Seuss Geisel, known as Dr. Seuss, to millions of children all over the world was born in Springfield, Massachusetts, in 1904.

B Theodor Seuss Geisel, known as Dr Seuss, to millions of children all over the world was born in Springfield, Massachusetts in 1904.

C Theodor Seuss Geisel, known as Dr. Seuss to millions of children all over the world was born in Springfield, Massachusetts, in 1904.

D Theodor Seuss Geisel, known as Dr. Seuss to millions of children all over the world, was born in Springfield, Massachusetts, in 1904.

2 **What is wrong with Sentence 2?**

F It contains a mistake in verb tense.

G It is a run-on sentence.

H It contains a mistake in punctuation.

J It is correct as it is.

3 **Which sentence contains a mistake in the use of adjectives?**

A Sentence 2

B Sentence 3

C Sentence 5

D None of them

4 **Which sentence contains an error in capitalization?**

F Sentence 1

G Sentence 5

H Sentence 6

J None of them

Answers

1 Ⓐ Ⓑ Ⓒ Ⓓ   **3** Ⓐ Ⓑ Ⓒ Ⓓ

18 **2** Ⓕ Ⓖ Ⓗ Ⓙ   **4** Ⓕ Ⓖ Ⓗ Ⓙ

Directions: Choose the sentence that is written correctly. Darken the circle for the correct answer.

Sample

A Demographers who are investigating the causes of human migration.

B One thing making migration possible, human beings having the tools and language to adapt to different conditions.

C As populations increased, distinctions between cultures evolved and, eventually, inequalities between cultures developed.

D Large groups of people who had been solely agricultural moving toward places where metal was found.

Directions: This is an article one student wrote for a history report. Before it can be turned in, however, some mistakes have to be corrected. Read the first paragraph of the article, and then answer the question. Darken the circle for the correct answer.

Child Labor in Great Britain

1. Some high school students complain about having to work part-time. 2. They would not complain near as much if they only had known what work was like for kids much younger than them during Great Britain's Industrial Revolution.

1 **Choose the best way to rewrite Sentence 2.**

A They would not complain near as much if they only knew what work was like for kids much younger than them during Great Britain's Industrial Revolution.

B They would not complain near as much if they only had known what work was like during Great Britain's Industrial Revolution for younger kids than them.

C They would not complain nearly as much if they only knew what work was like for kids much younger than they during Great Britain's Industrial Revolution.

D They would not complain nearly as much if they only had known what work was like for kids much younger then them during Great Britain's Industrial Revolution.

Answers

S   Ⓐ Ⓑ Ⓒ Ⓓ

1   Ⓐ Ⓑ Ⓒ Ⓓ

Directions: Read the next paragraph of the article. Darken the circle for the correct answer.

¹· Owners of cotton mills took orphans and children of poor parents to work in their factories. ²· This happened in the late 1700s. ³· The owners did not really pay the children, instead they paid only the cost of maintaining their young workers. ⁴· Children in the worst cases of five and six years of age had to work from thirteen to sixteen hours a day.

2 **Choose the best way to combine Sentences 1 and 2.**

F Owners of cotton mills took orphans and children of poor parents in the late 1700s to their factories to work.

G In the late 1700s, owners of cotton mills took orphans and children of poor parents to their factories to work.

H Owners of cotton mills took orphans and children of poor parents to their factories to work; this happened in the late 1700s.

J Owners of cotton mills took orphans and children of poor parents to their factories to work, and this happened in the late 1700s.

3 **What is wrong with Sentence 3?**

A It is not a complete sentence.

B It is unclear what "they" refers to.

C It is a run-on sentence.

D It is correct as it is written.

4 **Choose the best way to rewrite Sentence 4.**

F In the worst cases, children of five and six years of age had to work from thirteen to sixteen hours a day.

G From thirteen to sixteen hours a day, children of five and six years of age had to work—in the worst cases.

H Children five and six years old had to work in the worst cases from thirteen to sixteen hours a day.

J Five- and six-year-old children had to work from thirteen to sixteen hours a day in the worst cases.

Level I

Here is the next paragraph of the report.

¹· Some of the children kept living with their parents while they worked in mills and factories. ²· Young children also worked in very dangerous environments such as mines. ³· Often with the approval and encouragement of political, social, and religious leaders. ⁴· Children who arrived late for work have money deducted from their pitiful small wages and were often punished. ⁵· Timekeeping was a problem for the many poor families whom could not afford a clock.

5 **What is wrong with Sentence 3?**

A It does not belong in this paragraph.

B It is not a complete sentence.

C The comma after *social* is not needed.

D It is correct as it is.

6 **Choose the best way to rewrite Sentence 4.**

F Children who arrived late for work had money deducted from their pitifully small wages and were often punished.

G Children, arriving late for work, had money deducted from their pitiful small wages and were often punished.

H Children arriving late for work would have had money deducted from their pitifully small wages and often would have been punished.

J Arriving late for work, children have money deducted from their pitiful small wages and are often punished.

7 **What is wrong with Sentence 5?**

A There is a mistake in the use of pronouns.

B It should begin the next paragraph.

C There is a mistake in subject-verb agreement.

D It is a run-on sentence.

Directions: Here is the final paragraph of the report.

1. For many decades, beginning in 1802, social reformers tried to get laws passed that would eliminate the worst abuses of the child-labor system. 2. In 1836 Lord Ashley made a speech to members of Parliament to persuade them to limit the number of hours children could work. 3. He reported what sixteen doctors, including a Dr. Loudon, believed—that children could work no more than ten hours a day without ruining their health. 4. One adult interviewed by a Parliamentary committee said, "in reality, there were no regular hours; masters and managers did with us as they liked." 5. Demands for reform steadily increased.

8 Choose the sentence that does **not** belong in the paragraph.

F Sentence 1

G Sentence 3

H Sentence 4

J Sentence 5

9 Which sentence contains an error in capitalization?

A Sentence 2

B Sentence 3

C Sentence 4

D None of them

10 Choose the best concluding sentence for the paragraph.

F The social ills of child labor included illiteracy and a dramatic number of diseased and crippled children.

G James Patterson, another adult interviewed by the committee, said that he worked in a mill from five in the morning until nine at night.

H Committee members talked to many adults who had worked in factories as children.

J Sadly enough, though, no legislation to improve the lives of child laborers was passed until 1878.

Directions: Read the passage below and answer Sample A.

Sample Passage

The body requires vitamin A for normal growth. In addition, epithelial cells (cells that form membranes that line body cavities) need vitamin A to remain healthy. A deficiency of vitamin A can affect one's skin and eyes. In the case of the latter, a severe lack of vitamin A affects the retina such that the eyes can no longer adapt to the dark.

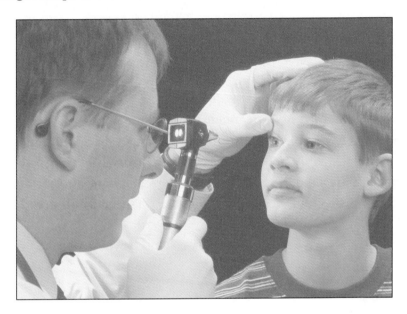

Sample A

What is the most likely source of this passage?

A a cookbook

B a dictionary

C an online encyclopedia

D a dictionary of scientific terms

Directions: A student wrote a report about vitamins and minerals. Here is an excerpt from his report. There are some mistakes that need correcting.

Sample B

¹· Vitamin A is a nonsoluble vitamin. ²· Which means that it is usually absorbed with foods containing fat. ³· By eating foods of animal origin such as milk and eggs, vitamin A can be obtained. ⁴· It is also obtained from eating green, orange, and yellow fruits and vegetables, such as carrots and bell peppers.

Choose the best way to combine Sentences 1 and 2.

F   Vitamin A, a nonsoluble vitamin, usually absorbed with foods containing fat.

G   Vitamin A is a nonsoluble vitamin; which means that it is usually absorbed with foods containing fat.

H   Usually absorbed with foods containing fat, vitamin A is a nonsoluble vitamin.

J   Vitamin A is a nonsoluble vitamin, which means that it is usually absorbed with foods containing fat.

Sample C

Choose the best way to write Sentence 3.

A   Vitamin A can be obtained by eating foods of animal origin, such as milk and eggs.

B   Animal origin foods such as milk and eggs gives you vitamin A.

C   You, by eating foods of animal origin, such as milk and eggs, can obtain vitamin A.

D   It is correct as it is.

Level I

Part 1

Eating to Live Well

Food is an essential part of our lives. Our bodies need it to function, grow, and thrive. Food provides us with the energy we need to think and move.

In the United States, there exists an amazing variety of foods—some of them less healthful than others. In this part, you will read about healthful and less healthful foods, foods that contain animal products and vegetable products, and foods that are especially good for your bones. You will also read about someone who has very definite ideas about the foods she eats.

Hippocrates, the Father of Medicine, suggested that your food should be your medicine and your medicine should be your food. This fifth-century B.C. Greek physician may have been right. Read the following article. Then do Numbers 1 through 7.

Can Milk Make You Happy? Can Fish Make You Smart?
by Faith Hickman Brynie

Food, Mind, and Mood: Three Examples

Imagine yourself lying in bed, your mind in turmoil. You toss and turn, but sleep won't come. Maybe a bedtime snack would help. What should you choose? If you think first of toaster waffles or popcorn, some experts would say you're on the right track. Foods high in complex carbohydrates—such as cereals, potatoes, pasta, crackers, or rice cakes—make many people relaxed and drowsy.

Missed that one? Try again. Suppose the weather's rotten, you forgot your homework, and your best friend is mad at you. What's good medicine when you're feeling low? A sugary cola or candy may give you a quick lift, but you'll crash just as quickly. Better choices may be Brazil

nuts (for selenium), skim milk (for calcium), or a spinach salad (for folic acid). In research studies, all three of those nutrients have been shown to lift spirits and battle the blues.

Try one more. You have a math test coming up in the afternoon. You want to be sharp, but you usually feel sleepy after lunch. Is your best choice an energy fix of fries and a shake or a broiled chicken breast and low-fat yogurt? If you pick the high-fat fries and shake, you may feel sluggish and blow that test. The protein-rich chicken and yogurt are better choices. Protein foods energize, some experts say.

Food and Brain

How does food affect mood and mind? The answer may lie in the chemistry of the brain and nervous system. Molecules called neurotransmitters are chemical messengers. They carry a nerve impulse across the gap between nerve cells. The release of neurotransmitter molecules from one neuron and their attachment to receptor sites on another keep a nerve impulse moving.

Nerve impulses carry messages from the environment to the brain—for example, the pain you feel when you stub your toe. They also carry messages in the other direction, from the brain to the muscles. That's why you back away from the obstacle that initiated the pain signal and exclaim, "Ouch!"

"Many neurotransmitters are built from the foods we eat," says neuroscientist Eric Chudler of the University of Washington. Too little or too much of a particular nutrient in the diet can affect their production, Chudler says. For example, tryptophan from foods such as yogurt, milk, bananas, and eggs is required for the production of the neurotransmitter serotonin. Phenylalanine from beets, almonds, eggs, meat, and grains goes into making the neurotransmitter dopamine.

Dozens of neurotransmitters are known; hundreds may exist. Their effects depend on their amounts and where they work in the brain. The neurotransmitter serotonin, for example, is thought to produce feelings of calmness, relaxation, and contentment. Drugs that prevent its reuptake (into the neuron that released it) are prescribed to treat depression. In at least some healthy, nondepressed people, carbohydrate foods seem to enhance serotonin production and produce similar effects. "It is the balance between different neurotransmitters that helps regulate mood," Chudler says.

Proper nutrition may also enhance brainpower. Choline is a substance similar to the B vitamins. It's found in egg yolks, whole wheat, peanuts, milk, green peas, liver, beans, seafood, and soybeans. The brain uses it to make the neurotransmitter acetylcholine. To test the effects of choline on memory and learning, researchers at the Massachusetts Institute of Technology gave memory tests to college students before increasing the amount of choline in their subjects' diets. Later, they retested. On the average, memories were better, and the students learned a list of unrelated words more easily.

1 **Which of these foods would be most effective in helping you feel calm and relaxed?**

A   spinach and soybeans

B   milk and bananas

C   almonds and meat

D   peanuts and seafood

2 **The article states, "Proper nutrition may also enhance brainpower."**

What is the best synonym of the word *enhance*, as it is used in the article?

F   decrease

G   affect

H   support

J   improve

3 **The author's purpose for writing the article is**

A   to test the reader's knowledge of nutrition

B   to describe ways that foods can affect the brain, nervous system, and mood

C   to provide a basic explanation of neurotransmitter action in the brain

D   to describe research efforts that have increased our knowledge of the food-nervous system relationship

4 Look at the following outline of this article. What belongs in C?

I.   Examples of foods affecting brain performance and mood

II.   Neurotransmitters

    A. Their relationship to nerve impulses

    B. Built from foods

    C. _____

    D. Neurotransmitters and brainpower

III. Conclusion

F Neurotransmitters and mood
G Carbohydrate foods
H Number of neurotransmitters
J How to feel calm and relaxed

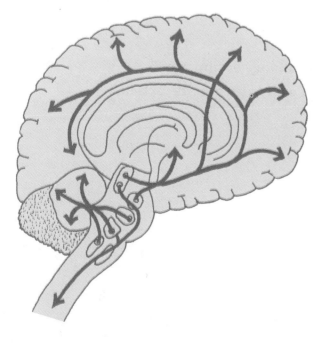

5 What did Massachusetts Institute of Technology researchers discover from the testing they did on college students?

A Students performed better on memory tests after the amount of choline in their diets was increased.

B The brain definitely uses choline to produce the neurotransmitter acetylcholine.

C Any memory task can be performed better after an individual consumes an increased amount of choline.

D People can learn a list of unrelated words with less difficulty if they eat more egg yolks and green peas.

6 In the first three paragraphs, what is the most probable reason that the reader is asked to make hypothetical choices about food?

F The author wants to begin with simple ideas and move on to more complex ones.

G The author wants to correct the reader's misconceptions about food.

H The author wants to interest the reader in the topic of the article.

J The author wants to provide clear reasons for later quoting experts in the field.

7 Which of these least supports the author's claim that people should choose healthful foods that nourish both body and mind?

A "Too little or too much of a particular nutrient in the diet can affect [neurotransmitters'] production."

B "Dozens of neurotransmitters are known; hundreds may exist."

C "A sugary cola or candy may give you a quick lift, but you'll crash just as quickly."

D "The neurotransmitter serotonin, for example, is thought to produce feelings of calmness, relaxation, and contentment."

Directions: Dietary guidelines issued by the United States Department of Agriculture can help people eat sensibly and nutritiously to stay healthy. Here is an explanation of one of the guidelines. Read the explanation and use it to help you do Numbers 8 through 11.

GUIDELINE: Foods high in fat should be used sparingly.

Some food groups in the Food Guide Pyramid are higher in fat than others. Fats and oils, as well as some types of desserts and snack foods that contain fat, provide calories but few nutrients. Many foods in the milk group and in the meat group (which includes eggs and beans, as well as meat, poultry, and fish) are also high in fat, as are some processed foods in the grain group. Choosing low-fat foods allows you to eat the recommended servings from these groups without going over your calorie needs.

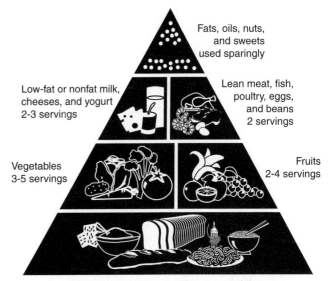

Fats, oils, nuts, and sweets used sparingly

Low-fat or nonfat milk, cheeses, and yogurt 2-3 servings

Lean meat, fish, poultry, eggs, and beans 2 servings

Vegetables 3-5 servings

Fruits 2-4 servings

Whole-grain bread, cereals, pasta and rice 6-10 servings

---

8 According to this guideline, what is the problem with some snack foods?

  F They are high in fat because they are processed.

  G They are full of calories but have little nutritional value.

  H There are too few low-fat options among them.

  J They are filling and will take the place of foods with more nutritional value.

9 Which is the best summary of the guideline's explanation?

  A It is important to know that not all foods in a food group are equally high in fat.

  B You should eat a variety of grain products, fruits, and vegetables.

  C You should avoid foods that provide you with calories but no nutrients.

  D It is best to choose the foods lower in fat in each of the food groups.

10 What is the most precise meaning of *nutrients* as it is used in the guideline's explanation?

  F low-fat sources of vitamins

  G varieties of nutrition

  H vitamins and minerals

  J nutritious substances in a food

11 Which one of these meals follows the guideline?

  A beans and rice, cornbread, orange

  B fried chicken, mashed potatoes with butter, carrot sticks

  C ham sandwich, chocolate chip cookies, low-fat milk

  D cheeseburger, french fries, vanilla ice cream cone

Directions: Here is part of an interview with a nutritionist about sugar consumption. Some of the words are missing. Choose the word that best fills each blank.

Did you know that sugar consumption in the United States has increased by 28 percent since 1983—and that the _____(12)_____ source of sugar in the average American's diet today is soft drinks? Most people in this country would do well to _____(13)_____ the amount of sugar they consume. And one simple way to achieve this is to drink low-fat or fat-free beverages such as milk, water, and fruit juices. Notice that I said fruit *juices*. Fruit "drinks" and fruit "beverages" have _____(14)_____ little nutritional value.

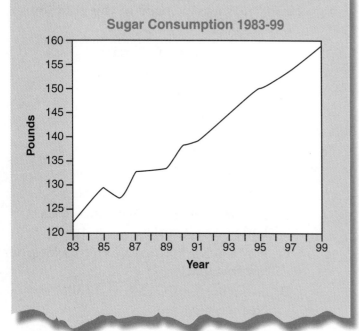

Sugar Consumption 1983-99

Pounds / Year

12 F predominant
     G pertinent
     H prudent
     J feasible

13 A quell
     B contemplate
     C enumerate
     D curtail

14 F inevitably
     G skeptically
     H deficiently
     J comparatively

15 **Which of these types of mistakes is <u>not</u> found in this sentence?**

> *Many health experts believes that including the amount of added sugars on a foods' packaging would help people reduce the amount of sugar they're eating and improve there diet.*

     A verb tense
     B use of apostrophes
     C subject-verb agreement
     D use of *there*, *they're*, and *their*

Directions: After reading the interview with the nutritionist about sugar consumption, Luisa decided to do some research on the topic. Here is a part of the report she wrote. There are some mistakes that need correcting.

1. The U.S. Department of Agriculture (USDA) recommends that people who eat a 2,000-calorie diet try not to consume more than 10 teaspoons of added sugars each day. 2. ("Added" sugars are added to the food; "natural" sugars are naturally found in the food.) 3. _____, the average American consumes 20 teaspoon of added sugars per day. 4. Many individual foods provide large fractions of the USDA's recommended sugar limit. 5. According to the USDA, people who have diets high in sugar consume less calcium, zinc, iron, and vitamins A, C, and E than people with diets lower in sugar.

16 **What is wrong with Sentence 2?**

F It contains an error in the use of quotation marks.

G It is a run-on sentence.

H The active voice instead of the passive voice should be used.

J It is correct as it is.

17 **Which of these is the best choice for the blank in Sentence 3?**

A On the other hand

B In addition

C However

D To the contrary

18 **Where would this sentence best fit in the paragraph?**

For example, a cup of regular ice cream provides 60 percent of the daily recommended amount of sugar, and a 12-ounce popular soft drink provides 103 percent.

F after Sentence 1

G after Sentence 3

H after Sentence 4

J after Sentence 5

Directions: Here is an interview with someone who has a particular perspective on food. Read the interview. Then do Numbers 19 through 26.

For the Love of Animals

An Interview with Vegetarian and Moosewood Cookbook Author Susan Harville

by Barbara Eagleshah

Twenty-seven years ago, a group of friends graduated from college and opened a vegetarian restaurant in the heart of downtown Ithaca, in upstate New York. Run as a collective, Moosewood Restaurant has been an unqualified success story. Now, nearly three decades later, the restaurant is more than twice its original size, is run by the corporation Vegetable Kingdom, has spawned seven cookbooks, and recently began marketing its own salad dressings. ODYSSEY spoke with one of Moosewood's original members, Susan Harville, about being a vegetarian.

In the cookbook *Sundays at Moosewood*, Susan tells the story of how she came to be involved in the restaurant, first as a waitress, and currently as cookbook author. It all began with a goat she bought from a local Finnish farmer. "Getting to know animals was the most fascinating and profound experience," she writes. "I acquired more animals. After a while I realized that if my friendship—my cosmic connection—to Freddy, Curley, and Loopy was to be respected, I had no choice but to become a vegetarian. Soon I was going to livestock auctions to outbid the buyers from meat-packing companies in order to rescue some veal calves to bring home."

Eventually she needed a job to help support her animals—400 in all!

ODYSSEY: How did you become involved with Moosewood?

Harville: The restaurant had been open just about a week when I started. It was certainly nothing I ever, ever planned as a career. I didn't even know how to cook. (Susan was an English major in college.) I wasn't a vegetarian yet. I had moved to a commune near Ithaca after graduate school. It was part of the "back to the land" movement.

ODYSSEY: When did you become a vegetarian?

Harville: I don't think I'd ever thought seriously about my diet. It was having animals that made me aware . . . they have friends, they have family, they have feelings. There are many reasons to become a vegetarian. But that is my reason. I think most kids today are far more aware of ecological issues, and their reasons for becoming vegetarian might be more sophisticated than mine were. Some don't want to hurt animals, and others are concerned about their own health or about the health of the planet.

ODYSSEY: What are some of the problems you experience as a vegetarian?

Harville: You encounter a lot of ignorance about what a vegetable product is, and what an animal product is. In your own family, you can deal with that. It becomes hard when you are a guest. Usually I try to say beforehand what my restrictions are—not that I expect the cook to change a menu for me—but I tell them ahead of time that I'm not going to eat things prepared with meat. This can be particularly hard for kids to do, because they are a little more socially awkward than adults are. It's not an easy thing. But my son (Emilio, 13) is not the least bit intimidated. He's always been a vegetarian.

ODYSSEY: Has your son ever tried eating meat?

Harville: No, he never has. I once said to him, "I bet when you get to be a teenager, you are going to rebel by eating a hamburger." He said he didn't think that was quite possible, because that would be like rebelling against yourself.

ODYSSEY: What changes at Moosewood have you seen in the last twenty-seven years?

Harville: When Moosewood first started, yogurt was weird! People had never heard of tabouli and hummus, things that are very common in delis now. It's much, much easier to be a vegetarian now than it was even twenty years ago. It's a whole different world out there in the grocery store. The same changes that you see in the food world in general are reflected here.

ODYSSEY: How do you ensure that you have a balanced diet as a vegetarian?

Harville: I think there is very little to worry about anymore. When Moosewood first started, we worried about "perfect proteins," about combining proteins so that we would have all of the amino acids that you might find in animal products. More recent findings are that you don't need to worry about combining protein in one meal, or even one day. As long as you are eating a variety of fruits and vegetables, plus beans and grains, you are going to get everything you need. In fact, in America, there is more of a problem with getting too much protein than there is with getting too little.

ODYSSEY: Do you have any parting advice for aspiring young vegetarians?

Harville: It's great if parents can help adolescent vegetarians. Even if parents can't help, there are several cookbooks out there, like *Vegetables Rock!: A Complete Guide for Teenage Vegetarians*, by Stephanie Pierson (Bantam Doubleday Dell, 1999). Also, kids can ask their schools to bring in programs like the Chefs' Collaborative's "Adopt a Chef" one. It's a program where chefs go into schools and teach about food, in a very deep sense. They teach about growing the foods, and about the cultures. It's not strictly vegetarian, but its focus is on ethnic foods and healthy foods. It makes you realize that you're not an outsider anymore. You're not a weirdo. You're a healthy person helping to make a healthier world.

19 According to Susan Harville, the current availability of unusual foods that do <u>not</u> contain animal products has resulted in

    A people in the United States reducing the amount of protein they consume

    B an increase in knowledge about what vegetable products are

    C vegetarians being able to eat as they wish with less difficulty

    D more teenagers becoming vegetarians

20 Which words or phrases from the interview are most effective in helping you identify the meaning of *intimidated*?

    F "not an easy thing" and "but"

    G "least bit" and "not an easy thing"

    H "socially awkward" and "least bit"

    J "particularly hard for kids" and "but"

21 Which conclusion can you draw from Susan Harville's answers in the interview?

    A It is difficult for adolescents to be vegetarians without the help of their parents.

    B Vegetarians must make sure they consume daily all the amino acids found in animal products.

    C Yogurt, tabouli, and hummus can now be found in almost every grocery store.

    D Relatively few Americans consume less protein than their bodies need.

22 Susan Harville said that, unlike herself, many of today's teenagers become vegetarians after taking into consideration

    F the treatment of animals raised for food production

    G their own health

    H the overabundance of proteins consumed by Americans

    J how readily available vegetable products are now

23 Of the following topics, which is the interviewer most interested in?

    A useful information for people who are or want to become vegetarians

    B why teenagers choose to become vegetarians

    C Susan Harville's involvement in a vegetarian restaurant

    D what Susan Harville's son has experienced as a vegetarian

24 **Which of these statements would Susan Harville most likely make?**

   F People must become better informed about the differences between vegetable and animal products.

   G More grocery stores need to stock foods that are free of animal products.

   H All teenagers should become more aware of ecological issues.

   J Vegetarians need a variety of fruits, vegetables, beans, and grains in their diets.

25 **This interview would most likely be found in a**

   A journal for nutritionists

   B magazine with a teenage readership

   C vegetarian cookbook

   D journal for restaurant owners

26 **Here are two sentences related to the passage:**

> *The Food Guide Pyramid was published by the USDA.*
>
> *Vegetarians who want to meet nutritional requirements can be helped by following the Food Guide Pyramid.*

Which of these best combines the two sentences into one?

   F The Food Guide Pyramid was published by the USDA, and vegetarians wanting to meet nutritional requirements can be helped by following the Food Guide Pyramid.

   G The USDA, which published the Food Guide Pyramid, can help vegetarians wanting to meet nutritional requirements.

   H Following the Food Guide Pyramid published by the USDA can help vegetarians who want to meet nutritional requirements.

   J Vegetarians, who want to meet nutritional requirements, can help by following the USDA's published Food Guide Pyramid.

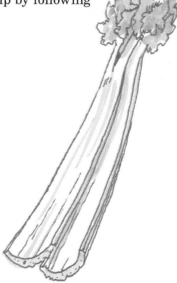

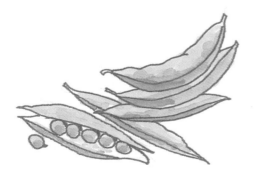

Directions: Here is the first paragraph of a report that Raymond wrote for his health class. There are some mistakes that need correcting.

1. I use to think that only older people needed to take care of their bones but now I realize I was'nt right. 2. My Aunt Lorraine, knowing what a serious athlete I am, gave me some advice about what I should be doing now to avoid problems later. 3. She's a Nutritionist who specializes in adolescent nutrition. 4. She graduated from the University of Massachusetts in 1994. 5. She told me that my body must have a certain amount of calcium to function properly; And if I don't get enough calcium from the foods I eat and drink my body will "rob" it from my bones.

27 Which sentence does <u>not</u> contain an error in capitalization?

  A Sentence 2

  B Sentence 3

  C Sentence 4

  D Sentence 5

28 Which sentence does <u>not</u> belong in the paragraph?

  F Sentence 2

  G Sentence 3

  H Sentence 4

  J They all belong in the paragraph.

29 Choose the best way to write Sentence 1.

  A I use to think that only older people needed to take care of their bones; but now I realize I wasn't right.

  B I used to think that only older people needed to take care of their bones, but now I realize I wasn't right.

  C I use to think that only older people needed to take care of their bones, but now I realized I wasn't right.

  D I used to think that only older people needed to take care of their bones but now I realize I was'nt right.

Level I

Directions: Raymond made a chart of information about calcium-containing foods. Use it to do Numbers 30 through 32.

SELECTED CALCIUM-RICH FOODS

Food Item (1 serving)	Dairy or Nondairy Source	Calcium (milligrams)	Calories
Almonds	nondairy	80	167
Broccoli (cooked)	nondairy	178	46
Cheese (American)	dairy	124	106
Milk (fat-free)	dairy	302	86
Milk (whole)	dairy	288	150
Orange juice (calcium-fortified)	nondairy	300	120
Salmon (including bones)	nondairy	181	118

30 The nondairy food listed in the chart that contains the greatest amount of calcium is

F   cooked broccoli

G   salmon

H   calcium-fortified orange juice

J   fat-free milk

31 Which of these conclusions can be drawn from the chart?

A   In general, nondairy foods provide less calcium than dairy foods do.

B   Cheese and whole milk contain too many calories for the number of milligrams of calcium they provide.

C   A serving of calcium-fortified orange juice and a serving of salmon will provide one's daily requirement of calcium.

D   Fat-free milk has both fewer calories and more calcium than whole milk.

32 Which food in the chart contains the smallest amount of calcium and the greatest number of calories?

F   almonds

G   American cheese

H   broccoli

J   salmon

33 Choose the sentence that best combines these two sentences into one.

The nutritionist interviewed two diabetic patients.

The nutritionist interviewed a man recovering from a heart attack.

A   The nutritionist interviewed a man recovering from a heart attack, also two diabetic patients.

B   The nutritionist interviewed two diabetic patients and a man recovering from a heart attack.

C   The nutritionist interviewed two diabetic patients and she interviewed a man recovering from a heart attack.

D   A man recovering from a heart attack and two diabetic patients were whom the nutritionist interviewed.

34 Here is another paragraph from the report Raymond wrote for his health class. Choose the sentence that best completes the paragraph.

> If my body "robs" calcium from my bones over a long period of time, my bones could become more fragile. If they're fragile, they'll fracture or break more easily. Aunt Lorraine told me something surprising about some teenagers who were active in sports for many years and weren't getting enough calcium: They suffered serious injuries because of how weak their bones had become. _____ .

F She said that weight-bearing exercise like jogging is also good for bones.

G Since I play soccer, basketball, and baseball, I really need to get enough calcium.

H Now I know that I need to build up a large amount of bone tissue.

J I'd like to find out which foods are highest in calcium.

35 Choose the topic sentence that best completes the paragraph.

> _____ . Most teenagers need at least 1,300 milligrams of calcium a day. A 1-ounce serving of hard cheese or an 8-ounce cup of milk or yogurt provides about 300 of those milligrams. Nowadays, foods like breakfast bars and fruit juices are being fortified with calcium. You can also get smaller amounts of calcium by eating salmon, almonds, and some dark green leafy vegetables.

A Getting enough calcium isn't that hard to do.

B Consuming enough calcium and doing weight-bearing exercises are important steps in bone health.

C Calcium is found in a variety of foods.

D My aunt told me about calcium in some of the foods I like to eat.

36 Which one of Raymond's sentences is grammatically correct?

F If a person is trying to consume fewer calories, they should avoid dairy products made with whole milk.

G I know many athletes at my school who will appreciate this information about calcium.

H My friend Roger and me both thought we didn't need to drink as much milk now that we are older.

J My aunt she has certainly straightened us out about our calcium needs.

Part 2

OUR TIES TO THE PAST

History is more than just lists of famous people and events and the dates associated with them. It includes the particular set of people and events that make up your own personal history. Because of your connection with the people and events that came before you, you are a bridge between the past and the future. This gives the past—especially the lives of your ancestors—much more meaning.

In this part, you will read narratives written by individuals who wanted to preserve memories of a special relative from an earlier generation. You will also read articles written by students who have begun exploring their unique pasts.

MY INDIAN GRANDMOTHER

by Charles A. Ohiyesa Eastman

As a motherless child, I always regarded my good grandmother as the wisest of guides and the best of protectors. It was not long before I began to realize her superiority to most of her fellow tribeswomen. I gained this idea from my own observation and from a knowledge of the high regard the other women had for her. Aside from her native talent and ingenuity, she had a truly wonderful memory. No other midwife in her day and tribe could compete with her in skill and judgment. She preserved in her mind, for later reference, all her observations as a midwife. And these observations were just as organized as if they had been written in a book.

I distinctly recall one occasion when she took me with her into the woods in search of certain medicinal roots. "Why do you not use all kinds of roots for medicines?" said I.

"Because," she replied, in her quick, characteristic manner, "the Great Mystery does not want us to find things too easily. In that case everybody would be a medicine-giver. Ohiyesa must learn that there are many secrets which the Great Mystery will reveal only to the most worthy. Only those who seek him fasting and in solitude will receive his signs."

With this and many similar explanations, she created in my soul wonderful and lively conceptions of the "Great Mystery" and of the effects of prayer and solitude. I continued my childish questioning.

"But why did you not dig those plants that we saw in the woods, of the same kind that you are digging now?"

"For the same reason that we do not like the berries we find in the shadow of deep woods as well as the ones which grow in sunny places. The latter have more sweetness and flavor. Those herbs which have medicinal value grow in a place that is neither too wet nor too dry. Such a place also receives a generous amount of sunshine.

"Someday Ohiyesa will be old enough to know the secrets of medicine. Then I will tell him all. But if you should grow up to be a bad man, I must withhold these treasures from you and give them to your brother. That is because a medicine man must be a good and wise man. I hope Ohiyesa will be a great medicine man when he grows up. To be a great warrior is a noble ambition. But to be a mighty medicine man is nobler!"

She said these things so thoughtfully and impressively that I cannot help but feel and remember them even to this day.

Our native women gathered wild rice, roots, berries and fruits. These formed an important part of our food. It was distinctively a woman's work. Uncheedah (grandmother) understood these matters perfectly. It became a kind of instinct with her to know just where to look for each edible variety and at what season of the year. This sort of labor gave the Indian women every opportunity to observe and study Nature after their fashion. In this, Uncheedah was more acute than most of the men. The abilities of her boys were not all inherited from their father. Indeed, the stronger family traits came obviously from her. She was a leader among the native women. They came to her not only for medical aid, but for advice in all their affairs.

In bravery she equaled any of the men. This trait, together with her ingenuity and alertness of mind, more than once saved her and her people from destruction. Once we were roaming over a region occupied by other tribes. On a day when most of the men were out hunting, a party of hostile Indians suddenly appeared. Although there were a few men left at home, they were taken by surprise at first and scarcely knew what to do. Then my grandmother came forward and advanced alone to meet our foes. She had gone some distance before some of our men followed her. She met the strangers and offered her hand to them. They accepted her friendly greeting; and as a result of her brave act we were left unmolested and at peace.

My father told me another story about her. My grandfather, who was a noted hunter, often wandered away from his band in search of game. In this instance he had with him only his own family of three boys and his wife. One evening, when he returned from the chase, he found to his surprise that she had built a stockade around her teepee. She had discovered the danger-sign in a single footprint, which she saw at a glance was not her husband's. She was convinced that it was not the footprint of a Sioux, from the shape of the moccasin. This ability to recognize footprints is general among the Indians, but more marked in certain individuals.

Once this courageous woman drove away a party of five Ojibway warriors. They had approached the lodge cautiously, but her dog gave timely warning. From behind her defenses she surprised them with the sound of gunfire, and the astonished braves thought it wise to retreat.

The Indian women, after reaching middle age, are usually heavy and lack agility. But in this also my grandmother was an exception. She was fully sixty when I was born. Yet when I was seven years old she swam across a swift and wide stream, carrying me on her back. She had not wished to expose me to an accident in one of the clumsy round boats of bull hide which were rigged up to cross rivers in our path. Her strength and endurance were remarkable. Even after she had reached the age of eighty-two, she one day walked twenty-five miles without appearing much fatigued.

When I consider the customs and habits of her people at the time, I marvel now at the purity and noble sentiment this woman possessed. She was descended from a proud chieftain of the "Dwellers Among the Leaves." When her husband died she was still comparatively a young woman—still active, clever, and industrious. Women of her age and position could remarry. In fact, she had several persistent suitors who were chiefs and men of her own age. Yet she preferred to cherish in solitude the memory of her husband.

solitude = state of being alone.

Make sure you are on Number 37 on your answer sheet.

37 This passage is most like

   A an autobiography

   B a short story

   C realistic fiction

   D an encyclopedia entry

38 Twice the narrator mentions his grandmother's *ingenuity*. What did he mean by this?

   F her bravery

   G her imagination

   H her cleverness

   J her genius

Directions: Use the web to answer Numbers 39 and 40.

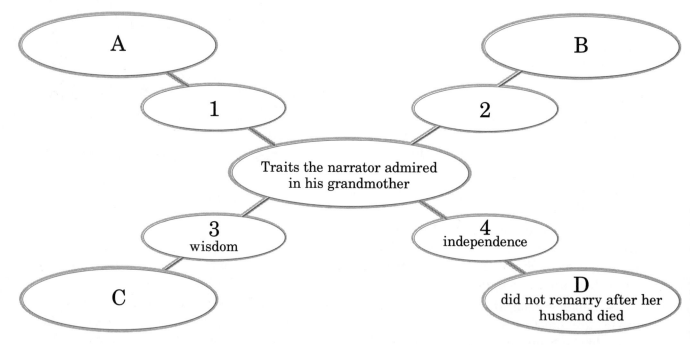

39 Which of these items are most appropriate for circles 1 and 2?

   A *aggressiveness* and *quick thinking*

   B *hunting ability* and *marksmanship*

   C *leadership* and *bravery*

   D *thoughtfulness* and *affection*

40 What should go in circles A, B, and C?

   F the importance of having this trait

   G a quote from the excerpt

   H another trait the narrator admired in his grandmother

   J a supporting fact from the excerpt

41 Which of these did the narrator not use to support his claim that his grandmother equaled any of the tribesmen in bravery?

A She went alone to greet a group of hostile Indians.

B She surprised and drove away enemy warriors with gunfire.

C She built a stockade around her family's teepee after recognizing the moccasin print of an enemy.

D She carried him on her back while swimming across a swift stream.

42 Which of these best explains why the grandmother's memory was of such great service to her?

F She was in charge of searching for medicinal plants, and she had to remember which were beneficial and which were harmful.

G She used it to retain the knowledge she had gained through observation.

H She needed it to "store" her observations until she could write them down in an organized fashion.

J She had to remember where edible plants could be located from one year to the next.

43 Which of these was probably most important to the narrator's grandmother?

A being the equal of men

B having a warrior grandson

C impressing tribespeople with her knowledge

D spending time in solitude

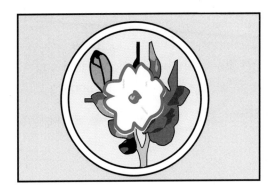

Flag of the Great Sioux Nation

44 **Which sentences best support this topic sentence?**

> *No people used their five senses better than we Indian children who were living in the wilderness.*

F We were so very free. Every day there was a real hunt. There was real game.

G It was the wilderness itself that was our teacher. The wilderness taught us to use each of our five senses.

H We were careful students of nature. We studied the habits of animals just as you study your books.

J We could smell as well as we could hear and see. We could feel and taste as well as we could see and hear.

45 **Choose the sentence that best fills the blank in the paragraph.**

It had been an especially good year for the Sioux. The spring fur hunters had been fortunate. Much maple sugar had been tapped. The women's patches of maize and potatoes were already sufficiently advanced to use. Now it was midsummer and time for celebration. The Wahpetonwan band of Sioux, the "Dwellers Among the Leaves," sent out invitations in the form of bundles of tobacco. _____. Turnips were dug up, and wild rice and ripe berries were gathered. An abundance of fresh meat was killed. Later, the ground was selected for the most important event, a lacrosse game between the two bands that had the greatest number of fast runners.

A After the other bands of Sioux had sent back their acceptances, preparations began for the feast.

B The other bands of Sioux sent back their acceptances, and then the athletic games were planned.

C Then attention was turned to planning the other events of the midsummer festivities.

D The feast was second in importance to the athletic games that were traditionally held.

46 Here is a paragraph from the narrative of a Native-American woman called Zitkala-Sa about her childhood. Choose the sentence that best completes the paragraph.

In the busy autumn days, Aunt Warca-Ziwin (which means "sunflower") came to our wigwam to help my mother preserve foods for our winter use. _____ . While my mother's hair was heavy and black, my aunt had unusually thin locks. Though my aunt was older than my mother, she was more jovial and less reserved. It was during my aunt's visits with us that my mother forgot her usual quietness, often laughing at some of her sister's clever remarks. I loved my aunt for three reasons: for her hearty laughter, for the cheerfulness she caused my mother, and most of all for the times she dried my tears and held me in her lap when my mother had scolded me.

F   There were few similarities in their physical appearance.

G   My aunt's personality had little in common with my mother's.

H   Although they were sisters, many things about them were quite different.

J   My aunt was almost, but not quite, as dear to me as my mother was.

47 Read the paragraph that Shaundra wrote in her journal. Choose the sentence that best completes the paragraph.

When I was little, Uncle Thomas always seemed like a gruff man. He sounded irate and impatient whenever he talked to us nieces and nephews. He rarely wanted to be around us. As I got older, though, I began to realize that my uncle actually had some wise things to say and some interesting stories to tell—especially about growing up in Los Angeles. Unfortunately, he passed away not long after I started enjoying his stories. _____ .

A   Another favorite of mine was his story about seeing three movie stars in one day.

B   I only wish that I had decided a few years earlier to really listen to what he had to say.

C   My uncle was great at describing places, and he could mimic people better than anyone else I knew.

D   I guess that all along he had really wanted to spend time with us kids.

Directions: Genealogy is the study of how a person descended from his or her ancestors. Many people take up genealogy as a hobby. Yvonne researched this topic and wrote an article about it for her school newspaper.

THE GIMBLE HIGH GAZETTE

Vol. 10, No. 6

Digging for Your Roots

◆ by Yvonne Fontaine

¹· Everyone says that us teenagers think only about the present and about ourselves. ²· Well, I'm a teenager and I like thinking about the past. ³· In particular, about past events that resulted in my being here today. ⁴· That's why I've become interested in genealogy, a fancy word that simply means studying your ancestors. ⁵· Since other Gimble High students might also be interested in digging for their roots (their ancestral roots, that is), I'm going to share some tips. ⁶· You might be looking for a hobby. ⁷· So put on your detective hat and get busy.

48 Which of these is the best way to write Sentence 1?

F Every one says that us teenagers think only about the present and about ourselves.

G Everyone says that we teenagers think only about the present and about ourselves.

H Every one says that us teenagers think only about the present and about us.

J Everyone says that we teenagers think only about the present and about us.

49 Which sentence is a run-on sentence?

A Sentence 2

B Sentence 4

C Sentence 5

D None of them

50 Which sentence does <u>not</u> belong in the paragraph?

F Sentence 2

G Sentence 3

H Sentence 6

J Sentence 7

51 Which sentence is a fragment?

A Sentence 3

B Sentence 6

C Sentence 7

D None of them

Now read the second half of Yvonne's article.

[1.] Start your search in familiar places. [2.] That means, first look for items in your own home and the homes of relatives. [3.] Things to look for include photos with names and dates on the back, letters, legal papers, school records, and baby books. [4.] See if one of your relatives have records of births, marriages, and deaths. [5.] Next, go to the nearest genealogy library or family history center. [6.] Staff members there will help you. [7.] Search obituaries (death announcements) in newspaper archives at your public library. [8.] Try to gain access to church and court records. [9.] Finally, investigate tombstone inscriptions since they sometimes include the place of origin of the deceased. [10.] You'll be amazed at how much fun learning a little history is when it has to do with *you*.

My Family Tree

Great Grandma Jones

Grandpa Jones   Grandma Jones   Grandpa Smith   Grandma Smith

Mom   Dad   Aunt Betty

Me

---

52 Where would this sentence best fit in the paragraph?

As an alternative, you may also be able to find information on the Internet.

F   after Sentence 2

G   after Sentence 3

H   after Sentence 6

J   after Sentence 9

53 What advice might Yvonne's journalism teacher have given her before she wrote this article?

A   Include at least a few words that will be new to your readers, but be sure you define them.

B   Make sure you provide complete details about each tip you present.

C   Keep the tips simple. There's no need to add additional information.

D   Motivate your readers with a lengthy introduction.

54 Choose the best way to combine Sentences 5 and 6.

F   Staff members will help you at the nearest genealogy library or family history center, where you should go next.

G   Go next to the staff members for help at the nearest genealogy library or family history center.

H   Next, go to the nearest genealogy library or family history center, staff members there will help you.

J   Next, go to the nearest genealogy library or family history center, where staff members will help you.

55 Which of the sentences contains an error in subject-verb agreement?

A   Sentence 3

B   Sentence 4

C   Sentence 9

D   None of them

Directions: After Yvonne's article was printed in the school newspaper, many students expressed an interest in doing genealogy research. They decided to ask the biology teacher to be the sponsor of a school chapter of the local genealogical society. Here is the application the teacher created that all students interested in joining the chapter would need to complete. Read the paragraph about one of the students wanting to join, and look carefully at the application. Then do Numbers 56 through 59.

Daniel Ortega lives with his aunt, Laura Benavides, who legally adopted him when he was two years old. Mrs. Benavides is an emergency room nurse at Samuel Green Memorial Hospital. His next closest family member is his grandfather, José Navarro, who lives two blocks away. Daniel is captain of the football team and volunteers once a week at the hospital where his aunt works. He has a paper route and mows lawns for his neighbor, Sarah Overton.

Gimble High School Chapter
of the Lewistown Genealogical Society

1. Date of application _____

2. Name of student _____ 3. ☐ Male ☐ Female

4. Date of birth _____ 5. Age _____

6. Address _____

7. Phone _____

8. Name of parent or guardian _____

9. Occupation of parent/guardian _____

10. Name and phone of parent/guardian's employer _____

11. Name and phone of a relative or friend to call if parent/guardian cannot be reached

_____

12. How long has your family lived in Lewistown?_____

13. What are your hobbies?_____

14. Which school activities/organizations do you participate in? _____

_____

15. (Parent/Guardian's signature) _____

56 **What should Daniel write on Line 9?**

F where his aunt works

G where his grandfather works

H what his aunt does for a living

J what he does to earn money

57 **Which line will Daniel not fill out?**

A Line 8

B Line 13

C Line 14

D Line 15

58 **What should Daniel write on Line 11?**

F José Navarro and his phone number

G Sam Green and his phone number

H Sarah Overton and her phone number

J Laura Benavides and her phone number

59 **What should Daniel write on Line 14?**

A high school football team

B hospital volunteer

C mow neighbor's lawn

D paper route

Directions: Dave Monahan joined the Gimble High School Chapter of the Lewistown Genealogical Society. Here is the first part of what he wrote for an assignment that the sponsor gave the organization's members. Some of the words are missing. Choose the word that best belongs in each blank.

Family Tree Investigation Results

It was with _____(60)_____ that I began this assignment: to investigate people in my family tree and write about my discoveries. Already knowing the answer, I asked my mother, "Wasn't anybody in our family even a *little* famous?"

"Not that I know of" was her response. Then, probably because of the _____(61)_____ look on my face, she told me I should talk to Uncle Stefan, whose hobby is genealogy. I called him that night and asked him the same question.

"What makes you so _____(62)_____ all of a sudden about your family?" he asked me. I explained my assignment and told him how much I'd like to write about a relative who wasn't _____(63)_____ .

"Well, there was 'Magic Lips' Cochran, my dad's brother. When he was young, he was a famous trumpet player in Chicago." This was great news because I play the trumpet too, and I intend to be famous one day.

60　**F**　chagrin
　　　　G　oblivion
　　　　H　quandary
　　　　J　vigilance

61　**A**　radical
　　　　B　despondent
　　　　C　nonchalant
　　　　D　boisterous

62　**F**　invincible
　　　　G　inquisitive
　　　　H　belated
　　　　J　genteel

63　**A**　tangent
　　　　B　unkempt
　　　　C　mediocre
　　　　D　ravenous

Directions: The following is a biographical sketch of Willa Cather. She is the author of the short story titled "A Wagner Matinée," an excerpt of which appears on pages 55 and 56. After you read this sketch and the excerpt, you should be able to identify a few elements common to both. Read the biographical sketch. Then do Numbers 64 through 67.

Willa Cather
(1873–1947)
by Susan Luton

Willa Cather spent the first nine years of her life in the South. She was born in 1873 near Winchester, Virginia, where her father raised sheep. Then, when Willa was an impressionable nine-year-old, her life took a drastic turn—a turn toward the West, to be exact. After their barn burned down, her father sold their property and uprooted his family. They moved to Webster County, Nebraska, to join Willa's paternal grandparents on their farm. Suddenly, she was surrounded by prairie grass instead of the Blue Ridge Mountains of Virginia.

The next year, Willa's father opened a real estate and loan office in Red Cloud. It was in that tiny Nebraska railroad town that she grew up and graduated from high school in 1890, along with her other two senior classmates. During the years she lived in Red Cloud, she was unconsciously absorbing the essential elements of the town, the rural surroundings, and their inhabitants. Much of the material in her later fiction was closely based on those essential elements.

However, neither rural nor small-town life must have appealed to her. A few months after graduating, she moved to Lincoln. While attending the University of Nebraska, she published several short stories in the university's literary magazine. In 1895, she graduated and returned to Red Cloud. Her stay was brief, though. Now an Eastern city attracted her. In 1896, she moved to Pittsburgh, Pennsylvania, to work as editor of a women's magazine.

Willa Cather spent the next ten years in Pittsburgh. After the magazine was sold in 1897, she began writing for a newspaper and publishing poems and short stories in several journals. She also taught high school Latin and English. Her first book, a collection of poems titled *April Twilights*, was published in 1903. Two years later, her first book of fiction, a collection of short stories called *The Troll Garden*, was published.

In 1906, Cather moved to New York City, which would remain her home for the remainder of her life. She had accepted an editorial position at *McClure's Magazine*, known for its investigative reporting of corruption in government and business. She also continued to write fiction. Her first novel, *Alexander's Bridge* (1912), and several early short stories were about artists and professionals and were set in London, Boston, and other cities. With the 1913 publication of *O Pioneers!*, however, it seems that she had begun to heed the advice of her friend Sarah Orne Jewett, a writer from Maine. Jewett had counseled Cather to write about the people, themes, and settings she had most taken to heart—all of which were a part of her past in Nebraska. The land of Nebraska, awe-inspiring and still wild in Cather's youth, is a setting, theme, and almost a character in *O Pioneers!* Two other well-received novels, *The Song of the Lark* (1915) and *My Ántonia* (1918), are also set in the Midwest and peopled with hardworking farmers and immigrants.

Much of Cather's later fiction reflects her gradual disillusionment with modern life. From her perspective, the heroic people who had settled the Midwest—and their way of life—were no longer to be found. They had been replaced with a new breed of people who had an exaggerated love of machines. A noble past had been destroyed.

During the last years of her life, Willa Cather continued to enjoy success with her public and critics. However, she suffered first from the deaths of friends and family members and later from her own failing health. She died of a cerebral hemorrhage in New York City in 1947.

64 **How did Cather's novels published from 1913 through 1918 differ from those that preceded and followed them?**

F   They portrayed her disappointment with modern life.

G   They reflected the most meaningful part of her past.

H   Their setting was mainly large cities.

J   They portrayed the wildlife of Nebraska.

Directions: Use the time line to do Numbers 65 through 67.

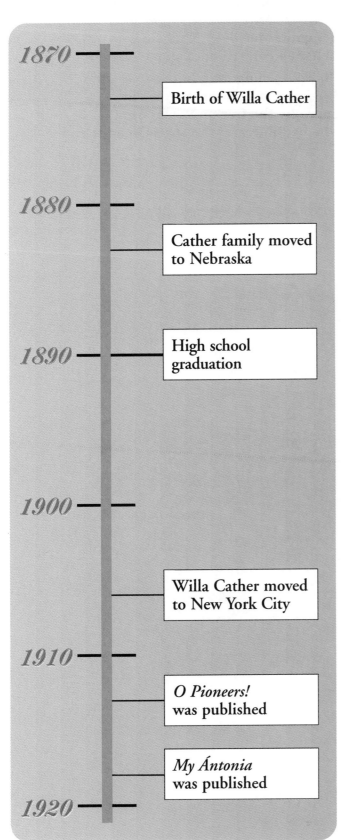

1870 — Birth of Willa Cather

1880 — Cather family moved to Nebraska

1890 — High school graduation

1900 —

Willa Cather moved to New York City

1910 —

O Pioneers! was published

My Ántonia was published

1920 —

65 Where would *"The Troll Garden* was published" appear on the time line?

   A midway between 1890 and 1900

   B midway between 1900 and 1910

   C just after 1910

   D just before 1920

66 All of these events would appear on the time line between 1890 and 1900 <u>except</u>

   F Willa Cather graduated from the University of Nebraska

   G Willa Cather wrote for a newspaper in Pittsburgh

   H Willa Cather's family moved to Red Cloud

   J Willa Cather became editor of a women's magazine

67 This time line is one way of organizing information from the passage. It would be most helpful to someone who

   A is interested in factors that influenced Willa Cather's writing

   B wants to learn details about Willa Cather's early life

   C is searching for a complete list of Willa Cather's works

   D wants to quickly see what the significant events in Willa Cather's life were

During her adult life, Willa Cather never lived in Nebraska. However, she remained close in spirit to the place. Her love for family members, especially those who had endured the rugged life of the Nebraska plains, might have been an influencing factor in her short story "A Wagner Matinée." This story appeared in *The Troll Garden*, her first published collection of short stories.

The narrator of "A Wagner Matinée" is Clark, a young man living in Boston. When Clark's aunt comes to his city for a business matter, he makes plans to take her to a matinée performance of an opera by the German composer Richard Wagner. The following excerpt is the beginning of the story. Read it and then do Numbers 68 through 75.

A Wagner Matinée

by Willa Cather

One morning I received a letter, written in pale ink on glassy, blue-lined note paper. It had the postmark of a little Nebraska village. This communication, worn and rubbed, looked as though it had been carried for some days in a coat pocket that was none too clean. It was from my Uncle Howard. It informed me that his wife had been left a small inheritance by a bachelor relative who had recently died. My aunt had to go to Boston to attend to the settling of the estate. He asked me to meet her at the train station and help her as needed. I discovered the date of her arrival to be no later than tomorrow.

The name of my Aunt Georgiana called up not only her own figure, at once pathetic and grotesque. But it also opened before my feet a gulf of recollection so wide and deep that I felt suddenly a stranger to all the present conditions of my existence. I felt wholly ill at ease and out of place amid the familiar surroundings of my study. I became, in short, the gangling farm boy my aunt had known, bashful, my hands cracked and sore from the corn husking. I felt the knuckles of my thumb, as though they were raw again. I sat again before her parlor organ, fumbling the musical scales with my stiff, red hands, while she, beside me, made canvas mittens for the huskers.

The next morning I set out for the station. When the train arrived I had some difficulty in finding my aunt. She was the last of the passengers to alight, and it was not until I got her into the carriage that she seemed really to recognize me. Her linen duster had become black with soot, and her black bonnet gray with dust, during the journey.

My Aunt Georgiana had been a music teacher at the Boston Conservatory, somewhere back in the late 1860s. One summer, while visiting in the little village among the Green Mountains, she had developed a fancy for Howard Carpenter, a handsome country boy nine years younger than she. When she returned to her duties in Boston, Howard followed her. The result of this unexplainable infatuation was that she eloped with him, avoiding the reproaches of her family and the criticisms of her friends by going with him to the Nebraska frontier. Carpenter, who, of course, had no money, had taken a homestead in Red Willow County, fifty miles from the railroad. They built a dugout in the red hillside, one of those cave dwellings whose inmates so often reverted to primitive conditions. Their water they got from the lagoons where buffalo drank, and their small stock of supplies was always at the mercy of bands of roving Indians. For thirty years my aunt had not been farther than fifty miles from the homestead.

The morning following her arrival she wore a black cotton dress, whose ornamentation showed that she had surrendered herself unquestioningly into the hands of a country dressmaker. My poor aunt's figure, however, would have presented astonishing difficulties to any dressmaker. Originally stooped, her shoulders were now almost bent together over her sunken chest. She wore ill-fitting false teeth. Her skin was as yellow as a Mongolian's from constant exposure to a pitiless wind and to the alkaline water that hardens the most transparent cuticle into a sort of flexible leather.

I owed to this woman most of the good that ever came my way in my boyhood, and I had a reverential affection for her. During the years when I was riding herd for my uncle, my aunt would cook the three meals—the first of which was ready at six o'clock in the morning. Then at night, after putting the six children to bed, she would often stand until midnight at her ironing board, with me at the kitchen table beside her, hearing me recite Latin. She would gently shake me when my drowsy head sank down over a page of irregular verbs. It was to her, at her ironing or mending, that I read my first Shakespeare. Her old textbook on mythology was the first that ever came into my empty hands. She taught me my music scales and exercises, too—on the little parlor organ, which her husband had bought her after fifteen years. During those first fifteen years she had not so much as seen any instrument, but an accordion that belonged to one of the Norwegian farmhands. She would sit beside me by the hour, darning and counting while I struggled with the "Joyous Farmer." But she seldom talked to me about music, and I understood why. Once I was doggedly beating out some easy passages from an old music score. She came up to me and, putting her hands over my eyes, gently drew my head back upon her shoulder. She said, "Don't love it so well, Clark, or it may be taken from you. Oh, dear boy, pray that whatever your sacrifice may be, it be not that."

68 **What is the mood of this excerpt?**

F lighthearted

G sentimental

H anxious

J hopeful

69 **Read what the aunt told her nephew in the last two sentences of the excerpt. What was she most likely thinking of when she said this?**

A her career as a music teacher

B the chores that constantly had to be done

C her love for her nephew

D her move from Boston to Nebraska

Level I

70 What does Clark mean precisely when he says that his aunt "had surrendered herself unquestioningly into the hands of a country dressmaker"?

   F His aunt must have lost an argument with the dressmaker about how her dress should look.

   G The dressmaker did not know how to style a dress for a woman with physical problems like those his aunt had.

   H The dressmaker needed to learn more about how to ornament dresses.

   J His aunt had trusted the skill of a less-than-qualified dressmaker.

71 According to Clark, what did his aunt expect to accomplish by *eloping* with Howard Carpenter?

   A She would move to a place where her husband could support her.

   B She would be with the man she loved.

   C She would not have to face negative reactions of her friends and family.

   D She would start a new life in an unfamiliar place.

72 Which of these is the least likely reason that Clark had a "reverential affection" for his aunt?

   F By having him husk corn, she taught him the value of hard work.

   G She helped him with his lessons after she had worked hard all day.

   H She introduced him to the world of music.

   J She gave him advice that was helpful to him as an adult.

73 Which of these best describes the aunt, based on clues found in the excerpt?

   A impatient; devoted to her husband

   B unselfish; accepting of her fate

   C strong-willed; nostalgic for her past

   D talented; content with her life

74 **Choose the question that is best answered by the following statement.**

> *His aunt made him feel like the young farm boy he used to be instead of the successful Bostonian that he now was.*

F Why did Clark say that it was to his aunt that he owed most of the good that came his way during his childhood?

G How did the aunt make Clark realize how far he has come in life?

H Why did Clark suddenly feel like a stranger in his own home?

J What was the effect on Clark of reading the letter from his Uncle Howard?

Directions: Use both the biographical sketch and the excerpt to do Number 75.

75 **Which of these details from her own life was Willa Cather least likely to have called upon as she was writing "A Wagner Matinée"?**

A She had lived in a rural setting in Nebraska.

B She had been a high school teacher in Pittsburgh.

C She had lived in large cities in the United States at the end of the nineteenth century.

D She had begun a new chapter of her life in a place very different from the one she had left.

Here is the first paragraph of a report that a student wrote after reading Willa Cather's "A Wagner Matinée." There are some mistakes that need correcting.

¹· My grandmother, my mother's Mother is a fascinating woman. ²· Her name is Hattie Marcum, and she is an excellent storyteller who is able to keep an audience spellbound for hours. ³· Why do I mention her when I am writing a report on Willa Cather's story called "A Wagner Matinée"? ⁴· There are two reasons Hattie Marcum tells wonderful stories about *her* grandmother who moved to Nebraska from the East Coast in 1881, and she was the one whom suggested that I read Cather's fiction.

76 **Which of these shows the best way to write Sentence 1?**

   F My Grandmother, my mothers Mother, is a fascinating woman.

   G My grandmother, my mothers mother is a fascinating woman.

   H My grandmother, my mother's Mother, is a fascinating woman.

   J My grandmother, my mother's mother, is a fascinating woman.

77 **Which of these is <u>not</u> true of Sentence 4?**

   A A colon is needed after *reasons*.

   B A comma is needed after *grandmother*.

   C The *whom* should be *who*.

   D *East Coast* should be lower-cased.

Now read the second part of the report and do Number 78.

In Cather's story, Aunt Georgiana left Boston and moved to Nebraska to start a new life with her new husband. My ancestor Sally Louise Marcum left Connecticut for Franklin County, just west of Webster County, the Cather family's destination. _____. Aunt Georgiana left behind a career as a piano teacher; Sally Louise had to leave her studies at a preparatory school in Hartford. In Nebraska, Aunt Georgiana and her husband grew corn, while the Marcum family raised cows and hogs.

78 **Which of these sentences best fills the blank in the paragraph?**

F In addition, Sally Louise lived in Nebraska with her husband, whom she met a few years later.

G However, Sally Louise moved to Nebraska with her family and met her husband, a railroad worker, a few years later.

H On the other hand, Sally Louise met her husband, a railroad worker, a few years after settling in Nebraska.

J Consequently, Sally Louise met her husband, a railroad worker, a few years later in Nebraska.

Now read the last paragraph of the student's report and do Numbers 79 and 80.

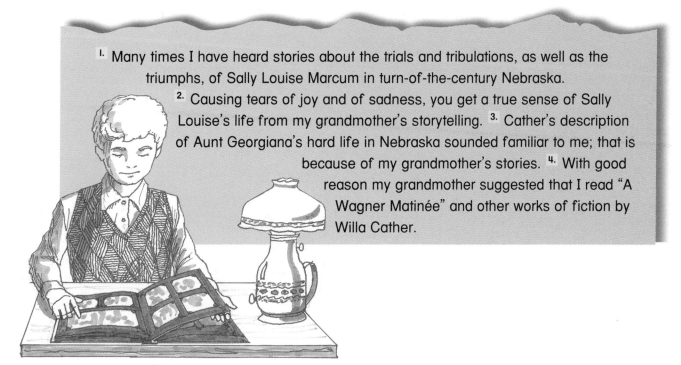

1. Many times I have heard stories about the trials and tribulations, as well as the triumphs, of Sally Louise Marcum in turn-of-the-century Nebraska. 2. Causing tears of joy and of sadness, you get a true sense of Sally Louise's life from my grandmother's storytelling. 3. Cather's description of Aunt Georgiana's hard life in Nebraska sounded familiar to me; that is because of my grandmother's stories. 4. With good reason my grandmother suggested that I read "A Wagner Matinée" and other works of fiction by Willa Cather.

79 What is the best way to write Sentence 1?

A Many times I have heard stories about the trials and tribulations as well as the triumphs of Sally Louise Marcum in turn of the century Nebraska.

B Many times I hear stories about the trials, tribulations, and triumphs, of Sally Louise Marcum in turn-of-the-century Nebraska.

C Many times I have heard stories about the trials, the tribulations as well as the triumphs, of Sally Louise Marcum in turn-of-the-century Nebraska.

D It is correct as it is.

80 Choose the best way to write Sentence 2.

F Causing tears of joy and of sadness, my grandmother's storytelling gives you a true sense of Sally Louise's life.

G You get a true sense of Sally Louise's life from my grandmother's storytelling, caused by tears of joy and of sadness.

H Causing tears of joy and of sadness gives you a true sense of Sally Louise's life from my grandmother's storytelling.

J It is correct as it is.

STOP

Answer Sheet

STUDENT'S NAME			SCHOOL:
LAST	FIRST	MI	TEACHER:

FEMALE ◯   MALE ◯

BIRTH DATE

MONTH	DAY		YEAR	
Jan ◯	⓪	⓪	⓪	⓪
Feb ◯	①	①	①	①
Mar ◯	②	②	②	②
Apr ◯	③	③	③	③
May ◯		④	④	④
Jun ◯		⑤	⑤	⑤
Jul ◯		⑥	⑥	⑥
Aug ◯		⑦	⑦	⑦
Sep ◯		⑧	⑧	⑧
Oct ◯		⑨	⑨	⑨
Nov ◯				
Dec ◯				

GRADE   ⑦ ⑧ ⑨ ⑩ ⑪ ⑫

T EST B EST for Success

(Name grid columns A–Z)

COMPREHENSIVE TEST: Reading and Language Arts

SA Ⓐ Ⓑ Ⓒ Ⓓ
SB Ⓕ Ⓖ Ⓗ Ⓙ
SC Ⓐ Ⓑ Ⓒ Ⓓ

1 Ⓐ Ⓑ Ⓒ Ⓓ
2 Ⓕ Ⓖ Ⓗ Ⓙ
3 Ⓐ Ⓑ Ⓒ Ⓓ
4 Ⓕ Ⓖ Ⓗ Ⓙ
5 Ⓐ Ⓑ Ⓒ Ⓓ
6 Ⓕ Ⓖ Ⓗ Ⓙ
7 Ⓐ Ⓑ Ⓒ Ⓓ
8 Ⓕ Ⓖ Ⓗ Ⓙ
9 Ⓐ Ⓑ Ⓒ Ⓓ
10 Ⓕ Ⓖ Ⓗ Ⓙ
11 Ⓐ Ⓑ Ⓒ Ⓓ

12 Ⓕ Ⓖ Ⓗ Ⓙ
13 Ⓐ Ⓑ Ⓒ Ⓓ
14 Ⓕ Ⓖ Ⓗ Ⓙ
15 Ⓐ Ⓑ Ⓒ Ⓓ
16 Ⓕ Ⓖ Ⓗ Ⓙ
17 Ⓐ Ⓑ Ⓒ Ⓓ
18 Ⓕ Ⓖ Ⓗ Ⓙ
19 Ⓐ Ⓑ Ⓒ Ⓓ
20 Ⓕ Ⓖ Ⓗ Ⓙ
21 Ⓐ Ⓑ Ⓒ Ⓓ
22 Ⓕ Ⓖ Ⓗ Ⓙ
23 Ⓐ Ⓑ Ⓒ Ⓓ
24 Ⓕ Ⓖ Ⓗ Ⓙ
25 Ⓐ Ⓑ Ⓒ Ⓓ

26 Ⓕ Ⓖ Ⓗ Ⓙ
27 Ⓐ Ⓑ Ⓒ Ⓓ
28 Ⓕ Ⓖ Ⓗ Ⓙ
29 Ⓐ Ⓑ Ⓒ Ⓓ
30 Ⓕ Ⓖ Ⓗ Ⓙ
31 Ⓐ Ⓑ Ⓒ Ⓓ
32 Ⓕ Ⓖ Ⓗ Ⓙ
33 Ⓐ Ⓑ Ⓒ Ⓓ
34 Ⓕ Ⓖ Ⓗ Ⓙ
35 Ⓐ Ⓑ Ⓒ Ⓓ
36 Ⓕ Ⓖ Ⓗ Ⓙ
37 Ⓐ Ⓑ Ⓒ Ⓓ
38 Ⓕ Ⓖ Ⓗ Ⓙ
39 Ⓐ Ⓑ Ⓒ Ⓓ
40 Ⓕ Ⓖ Ⓗ Ⓙ

41 Ⓐ Ⓑ Ⓒ Ⓓ
42 Ⓕ Ⓖ Ⓗ Ⓙ
43 Ⓐ Ⓑ Ⓒ Ⓓ
44 Ⓕ Ⓖ Ⓗ Ⓙ
45 Ⓐ Ⓑ Ⓒ Ⓓ
46 Ⓕ Ⓖ Ⓗ Ⓙ
47 Ⓐ Ⓑ Ⓒ Ⓓ
48 Ⓕ Ⓖ Ⓗ Ⓙ
49 Ⓐ Ⓑ Ⓒ Ⓓ
50 Ⓕ Ⓖ Ⓗ Ⓙ
51 Ⓐ Ⓑ Ⓒ Ⓓ
52 Ⓕ Ⓖ Ⓗ Ⓙ
53 Ⓐ Ⓑ Ⓒ Ⓓ
54 Ⓕ Ⓖ Ⓗ Ⓙ
55 Ⓐ Ⓑ Ⓒ Ⓓ

56 Ⓕ Ⓖ Ⓗ Ⓙ
57 Ⓐ Ⓑ Ⓒ Ⓓ
58 Ⓕ Ⓖ Ⓗ Ⓙ
59 Ⓐ Ⓑ Ⓒ Ⓓ
60 Ⓕ Ⓖ Ⓗ Ⓙ
61 Ⓐ Ⓑ Ⓒ Ⓓ
62 Ⓕ Ⓖ Ⓗ Ⓙ
63 Ⓐ Ⓑ Ⓒ Ⓓ
64 Ⓕ Ⓖ Ⓗ Ⓙ
65 Ⓐ Ⓑ Ⓒ Ⓓ
66 Ⓕ Ⓖ Ⓗ Ⓙ
67 Ⓐ Ⓑ Ⓒ Ⓓ
68 Ⓕ Ⓖ Ⓗ Ⓙ
69 Ⓐ Ⓑ Ⓒ Ⓓ
70 Ⓕ Ⓖ Ⓗ Ⓙ

71 Ⓐ Ⓑ Ⓒ Ⓓ
72 Ⓕ Ⓖ Ⓗ Ⓙ
73 Ⓐ Ⓑ Ⓒ Ⓓ
74 Ⓕ Ⓖ Ⓗ Ⓙ
75 Ⓐ Ⓑ Ⓒ Ⓓ
76 Ⓕ Ⓖ Ⓗ Ⓙ
77 Ⓐ Ⓑ Ⓒ Ⓓ
78 Ⓕ Ⓖ Ⓗ Ⓙ
79 Ⓐ Ⓑ Ⓒ Ⓓ
80 Ⓕ Ⓖ Ⓗ Ⓙ